Travel

Ksamil, ALBANIA

The Must-Have Travel Companion for Your Adventure!

Wybikes Hinton

COPYRIGHT NOTICE

This publication is copyright protected. This is only for personal use. No part of this publication may be, including but not limited to, reproduced, in any form or medium, stored in a data retrieval system or transmitted by or through any means, without prior written permission from the Author / Publisher.

Legal action will be pursued if this is breached.

DISCLAIMER

Please note that the information contained within this document is for educational purposes only. The information contained herein has been obtained from sources believed to be reliable at the time of publication. The opinions expressed herein are subject to change without notice.

Readers acknowledge that the Author / Publisher is not engaging in rendering legal, financial or professional advice. The Publisher / Author disclaims all warranties as to the accuracy, completeness, or adequacy of such information.

The Publisher assumes no liability for errors, omissions, or inadequacies in the information contained herein or from the interpretations thereof. The publisher / Author specifically disclaims any liability from the use or application of the information contained herein or from the interpretations thereof.

TABLE OF CONTENT

Copyright Notice ii
Disclaimer iii
Table of Content iv
Introduction 10
Welcome To KSAMIL ALBANIA 10
   About This Travel Guide 10
   Why Ksamil? 11
   How to Use This Guide 12

Chapter 1 14
Introduction to Ksamil 14
   Geographic Overview 14
   Historical Background 15
   Cultural Significance 16

Chapter 2 18
Getting Started with Your Trip 18
   Planning for Your Journey 18
   Travel Documents and Requirements 20
   Transportation Options 21

Chapter 3 23
Accommodation in Ksamil 23
   Overview of Accommodation Options 23
   Luxury Resorts 25
   Budget-Friendly Hotels 26

    Boutique Guesthouses 29
    Unique Stays 32
    Top Recommended Accommodation 35
    Choosing the Right Accommodation for You 38
    Booking Tips and Tricks 41

Chapter 4 44
Exploring Ksamil 44
    Beaches and Coastline 44
    Natural Attractions. 47
    Parks and Gardens 49

Chapter 5 53
Cuisine and Dining 53
    Traditional Albanian Dishes 53
    Local Seafood Specialties 56
    Dining Etiquette & Tips 58

Chapter 6 61
Shopping and Markets 61
    Souvenirs and Handicrafts 61
    Local Markets and Bazars 64
    Shopping Districts 66

Chapter 7 70
Nightlife and Entertainment 70
    Bars and Cafés 70
    Night Clubs and Lounges 73
    Cultural Performances 75

Chapter 8 78
Outdoor Activities 78
    Water Sports 78
    Hiking & Trekking Trails 81
    Cycling Routes 83

Chapter 9 86
Day Trips and Excursions 86
    Butrint National Park 86
    Blue Eye Spring 89
    Saranda City Tour 91

Chapter 10 94
Historical and Cultural Sites 94
    Butrint Archaeological Site 94
    Ancient Ruins and Monuments 96
    Museums and Galleries 98

Chapter 11 102
Local Festivals and Events 102
    Summer Festivals 102
    Religious Celebrations 105
    Folklore Events 107

Chapter 12 111
Health and Safety Tips 111
    Emergency Contacts 111
    Medical Facilities 113
    Travel Insurance 114

Chapter 13 117
Language and Communication 117
- Basic Albanian Phrases 117
- Language Tip for Tourists 118
- Communication Etiquette 120

Chapter 14 122
Itineraries and Sample Plans 122
- Weekend Getaway 122
- Cultural Immersion 125
- Outdoor Adventure 128
- Family-Friendly Trip 132
- Budget Travel 137
- Solo Traveler's Guide 141
- Romantic Getaways 145

Chapter 15 149
Transportation within Ksamil 149
- Public Transportation 149
- Rental Services 151
- Taxi Services 152

Chapter 16 154
Ecotourism and Sustainability 154
- Environmental Conservation Efforts 154
- Environmentally Friendly Practices 156
- Responsible Tourism Tips 158

Chapter 17 160
Family-Friendly Activities 160

    Children-Friendly Attractions 160

    Family-oriented Services 162

    Safety Precautions for Families 163

Chapter 18 166
Relaxation and Wellness 166

    Spa and Wellness Centers 166

    Yoga and Meditation Retreats 168

    Beach Relaxation Tips 170

Chapter 19 172
Photography and Sightseeing Tips 172

    Scenic Spots and Photography Opportunities 172

    Photographic Guidelines 174

    Must-see Landmarks 176

Chapter 20 178
Local Customs and Traditions 178

    Etiquette and Manners 178

    Traditional Practices 180

    Cultural Sensitivity 182

Chapter 21 185
Traveling on a Budget 185

    Budget-Friendly Accommodation 185

    Affordable Dining Options 186

    Free or low-cost activities 188

Chapter 22 190
Conclusion and Final Tips 190

Summary of Key Highlights 190
Last Minute Recommendations 192
Feedback and Suggestions 193

Appendix 195
Useful Resources 195

Emergency Contacts 195
Maps and Navigational Tools 196
Additional Reading and References 196
Useful Local Phrases 197
Addresses and Locations for Popular Accommodation 198
Addresses and Locations for Popular Restaurants and Cafes 199
Addresses and Locations for Popular Bars and Clubs 200
Addresses and locations of major attractions 201
Map of Ksamil, Albania 203
Map of Restaurants 204
Map of Things to Do in Ksamil 205
Map of Museums 206

Introduction

WELCOME TO KSAMIL ALBANIA

Ah, Ksamil! Nestled along the gorgeous Albanian Riviera, this hidden gem is waiting to be discovered. Ksamil, with its magnificent beaches, rich history, and dynamic culture, guarantees a wonderful experience for all visitors. Whether you want to relax by the blue waves or immerse yourself in the local culture, Ksamil has a plethora of activities waiting to be explored.

About This Travel Guide

In this detailed travel guide, we want to be your reliable companion on your trip to Ksamil. This guide is full of insider ideas, insightful insights, and practical guidance to help you improve your travel experience and make the most of your stay in this lovely region.

Our staff has painstakingly compiled this guide to present you with all you need to know, from organizing your vacation and discovering Ksamil's hidden gems to delighting in local food and enjoying the lively culture. Whether you're a seasoned traveler or starting on your first excursion, this guide is designed to match your needs and provide a seamless and engaging travel experience in Ksamil.

Why Ksamil?

You might be wondering why you should use Ksamil among the various other options available. The answer is found in the exceptional beauty and charm that characterize this seaside paradise.

Ksamil has some of the most beautiful beaches on the Albanian Riviera, with pure white sands and clear seas that attract visitors from all over the world. Whether lazing in the sun on Pasqyra Beach or exploring the Ksamil Islands' secret coves, every time spent by the water demonstrates Ksamil's natural charms.

Beyond its stunning shoreline, Ksamil is rich in history and culture. Every aspect of Ksamil offers a narrative of perseverance and tradition, from the ancient remains of Butrint National Park to the tiny towns that dot the shoreline. Wander through cobblestone alleyways, sample traditional specialties, and interact with friendly residents to immerse yourself in the vivid tapestry of Albanian heritage.

In Ksamil, time appears to slow down, urging you to accept the relaxed pace of life and cherish every minute. Whether you're looking for adventure or relaxation, cultural immersion, or gastronomic pleasures, Ksamil has something for everyone.

How to Use This Guide

Navigating through the abundance of information presented in this book may appear daunting at first look. However, do not worry! We've designed this guide to be simple and accessible, allowing you to plan and execute your Ksamil excursion without difficulty.

Here's a quick summary of how to get the most out of this guide:

- **Navigate Easily:** Use the table of contents to find the information you need easily. Whether you're organizing your schedule or looking for restaurant and lodging recommendations, our well-organized structure ensures that useful information is always just a click away.
- **Discover Comprehensive Insights:** Delve into each chapter to find thorough insights and insider recommendations on all elements of Ksamil tourism.

From lodging alternatives and transit advice to cultural etiquette and safety considerations, we've got you covered.
- **Personalize Your Experience:** Customize your Ksamil experience to reflect your interests and preferences. Whether you enjoy the beach, history, or gastronomy, our guide has a variety of ideas and suggestions to ensure a tailored and unforgettable trip.
- **Engage with Local Resources:** Use the guide's resources to learn more about Ksamil's culture, history, and environment. From language lessons and cultural etiquette to eco-tourism programs and volunteer opportunities, we invite you to interact with the local population and positively impact the area.
- **Embrace Spontaneity:** While careful planning is necessary for a successful travel experience, don't forget to allow for spontaneity and discovery. Allow yourself to explore off the usual road, mingle with locals, and find hidden gems that guidebooks may not cover.

With these recommendations in mind, go off on your adventure to Ksamil with confidence and curiosity. Allow this seaside haven's stunning vistas, rich tradition, and kind hospitality to captivate your senses and leave you with unforgettable memories.

Chapter 1

INTRODUCTION TO KSAMIL

Ksamil, a lovely seaside community tucked along the Albanian Riviera, enchants visitors with its breathtaking scenery, rich history, and dynamic culture.

In this chapter, we will look at Ksamil's geography, history, and cultural importance, providing insights into what makes this location so special.

Geographic Overview

Ksamil is located in southern Albania, on the Ionian shore, about 15 kilometers south of Sarandë. Its strategic location near the Greek border, as well as its closeness to the Ionian Sea, makes it an ideal destination for both beachgoers and historians

Ksamil is known for its gorgeous beaches, crystal blue seas, and lush foliage. The coastline is dotted with quiet coves, rocky outcrops, and tiny islands, providing a stunning backdrop for those seeking peace and natural beauty.

The climate of Ksamil is Mediterranean, with hot, dry summers and warm, rainy winters. The summer months, from June to August, are the most popular with tourists since they provide great weather for beach sports and outdoor adventures. The pleasant sea wind gives relief from the heat, making it ideal for sunbathing and water activities.

Historical Background

Ksamil's history spans thousands of years, with traces of human occupancy reaching back to the Bronze Age. Throughout history, Ksamil has been impacted by different civilizations, including the Ancient Greeks, Romans, Byzantines, and Ottomans, each of whom left their stamp on the region's cultural legacy.

Butrint National Park, a UNESCO World Heritage Site, is one of Ksamil's most important historical monuments, known for its well-preserved ruins and archeological treasures. Butrint, located near Ksamil, was an important commercial hub and village in antiquity, with a rich history spanning over 2,500 years.

The ruins of Butrint provide a look into the past, with vestiges of old temples, theaters, and fortresses shedding light on the region's turbulent history. Butrint has been molded by various civilizations, from Greek and Roman to Byzantine and Venetian, each adding to its cultural and architectural legacy.

Cultural Significance

Ksamil has enormous cultural value as a melting pot of many cultures and customs. The village's closeness to the Mediterranean Sea has had a significant impact on its cultural character, with nautical activities and fishing traditions profoundly embedded in the local way of life.

Ksamil residents are noted for their warmth and generosity, eagerly welcome guests, and proudly present their rich cultural history. Traditional Albanian customs and rituals are observed all year, allowing both residents and tourists to take part in age-old traditions and festivals.

Religion also plays an important role in Ksamil's cultural environment, with mosques and churches acting as symbols of faith and belonging. The settlement has a mixed religious population, reflecting Albania's tradition of religious tolerance and harmony.

Throughout the year, Ksamil hosts a variety of cultural events and festivals that celebrate the region's unique arts, music, and culinary traditions. These events provide a look into the heart and soul of Ksamil's cultural history, including traditional dances and music performances as well as gourmet pleasures highlighting local specialties.

In essence, Ksamil is more than simply a tourist attraction; it is a monument to the lasting spirit of its people, as well as the rich tapestry of history and culture that distinguishes this wonderful part of the globe. As you go to Ksamil, expect to be immersed in a world of natural beauty, historical intrigue, and cultural variety that will make an indelible mark on your spirit.

Chapter 2

GETTING STARTED WITH YOUR TRIP

Traveling to Ksamil involves considerable planning and preparation to ensure a smooth and pleasurable visit.

In this chapter, we look at the fundamental procedures for getting started on your trip, such as planning your excursion, understanding travel paperwork and regulations, and researching transportation alternatives to get to your destination.

Planning for Your Journey

Preparing for your vacation to Ksamil begins far before you set foot on Albanian territory. Here are some important actions to guarantee a flawless travel experience:

- **Research and Planning:** Become acquainted with Ksamil's attractions, climate, and culture. To adapt

your schedule to your interests and tastes, look at different types of lodging, activities, and attractions.
- **Health and Safety Precautions**: Check with your doctor to make sure you are up to date on the vaccines and prescriptions advised for travel to Albania. Consider obtaining travel insurance to protect against unanticipated medical problems or trip cancellations.
- **Packing Essentials**: Create a packing list depending on the activities you intend to conduct in Ksamil. Sunscreen, swimsuits, suitable walking shoes, lightweight clothes for hot weather, bug repellant, and any medications or toiletries you may require are all essentials.
- **Currency and Banking:** Familiarize yourself with the Albanian Lek (ALL) and its exchange rates. Consider bringing both cash and credit/debit cards for convenience, and advise your bank of your trip intentions to avoid any card usage complications while overseas.
- **Communication:** To stay connected during your journey, set up international roaming or get a local SIM card when you arrive in Albania. Make a list of vital contact numbers, such as emergency services, your lodging, and local transit providers.

Travel Documents and Requirements

Before traveling to Ksamil, make sure you have the proper travel papers and satisfy the entrance criteria for Albania.

Passport: Ensure that your passport is valid for at least six months beyond your intended departure date from Albania. Renew your passport if necessary to prevent problems at immigration.

- **Visa:** Citizens of numerous countries, including the United States, Canada, and European Union member states, can enter Albania without a visa for short periods of up to 90 days. However, before traveling, make sure to verify the visa requirements for your nationality.
- **Entry Requirements:** If questioned by immigration officials upon arrival, bring documentation of onward travel and sufficient finances to cover your stay in Albania.
- **COVID-19 procedures**: Be aware of any COVID-19-related travel restrictions, testing requirements, or quarantine procedures that may be in effect for passengers entering Albania. Before you go, make sure to check the latest updates from Albanian authorities and international health groups.

Transportation Options

Getting to Ksamil entails investigating numerous transportation choices, each with its benefits and considerations:

- **Air Travel:** The nearest international airport to Ksamil is Tirana International Airport Nënë Tereza (TIA), located roughly 220 kilometers north. Domestic flights, private transfers, and rental vehicles are all options for getting to Ksamil from Tirana.
- **Ground Transportation:** For those arriving by plane, ground transportation options from Tirana to Ksamil include buses, private shuttles, and rental vehicles. The drive takes around four to five hours, depending on traffic and road conditions, and provides stunning vistas of the Albanian countryside.
- **Public Transportation:** Once in Ksamil, buses, minibusses, and taxis are available to get about the hamlet and its surroundings. While buses are typically inexpensive and dependable, renting a vehicle or scooter provides more flexibility and convenience for exploring the area at your leisure.
- **Ferry Services:** Travelers traveling from Corfu, Greece can take a ferry from Corfu Town to Sarandë, which is

about 15 kilometers north of Ksamil. From Sarandë, take a cab or bus to Ksamil in less than 30 minutes.
- **Driving Considerations:** If you intend to hire a car in Albania, become acquainted with local traffic rules, road signs, and driving practices. Be prepared for limited roads, steep terrain, and occasional cattle crossings, particularly in rural settings.

Understanding your travel documents, planning for your trip, and researching transportation choices will help you plan a wonderful and hassle-free vacation in Ksamil. As you begin your journey, embrace the spirit of exploration and discovery, and allow yourself to be swept away by the beauty and charm of this wonderful seaside region.

Chapter 3

ACCOMMODATION IN KSAMIL

Finding the right hotel is an important part of arranging your vacation to Ksamil.

In this chapter, we will look at the various accommodations available in Ksamil, ranging from luxurious resorts to lovely guesthouses.

Overview of Accommodation Options

Ksamil offers a diverse range of lodging alternatives, from luxury resorts and boutique hotels to low-cost guesthouses and rental flats. Whatever your budget or travel style, you'll find the ideal location to stay in Ksamil.

- **Luxury Resorts:** For travelers seeking unparalleled comfort and indulgence, Ksamil's luxury resorts offer opulent amenities, stunning views, and world-class service.

- **Boutique Hotels:** Boutique hotels in Ksamil provide intimate and beautiful lodgings, generally with distinctive décor, customized service, and lovely settings.
- **Guesthouses and Bed and Breakfasts**: Experience Albanian hospitality at its finest by staying in one of Ksamil's guesthouses or bed and breakfast establishments. These comfortable lodgings provide a home-away-from-home feel, complete with warm greetings and delicious meals.
- **Rental Villas and Apartments:** Rental villas and apartments in Ksamil are ideal for families or groups of friends, offering spacious and private lodgings equipped with kitchens, living areas, and outdoor spaces.
- **Camping Sites:** Nature lovers may immerse themselves in the great outdoors by staying at one of Ksamil's authorized camping areas. Wake up to the sounds of songbirds and the soft rustle of leaves in a setting of pristine natural beauty.

Regardless of the type of accommodation you choose, Ksamil's housing options promote comfort, convenience, and unique experiences, ensuring that each visitor has a wonderful stay.

Luxury Resorts

Luxury resorts in Ksamil provide the best in comfort for guests seeking leisure and enjoyment. With opulent amenities and beautiful vistas, these resorts take the vacation experience to new heights.

- **The Five-Star Experience:** Ksamil's luxury resorts include five-star amenities and services, such as beautiful lodgings, gourmet cuisine, spa facilities, and individual concierge services. Whether you're lazing by the pool, enjoying in a soothing spa treatment, or eating a scrumptious dinner made by world-class chefs, every moment is intended to exceed your expectations.
- **Breathtaking Locations:** Luxury resorts located along Ksamil's pristine beachfront provide stunning views of the Ionian Sea and neighboring scenery. Wake up to the sound of waves smashing against the coast and watch beautiful sunsets paint the sky in orange and pink from your private balcony or patio.
- **Exquisite Dining:** Dining at a luxury resort in Ksamil is a gourmet adventure in itself. Indulge your taste buds with a broad menu of delicious meals influenced by Mediterranean tastes and locally produced ingredients. From high dining establishments to simple seaside cafés, every meal is a work of art designed to satisfy the senses.

- **World-Class Amenities:** When it comes to guest amenities and services, luxury resorts in Ksamil go above and beyond. Enjoy access to cutting-edge fitness facilities, infinity pools, private beaches, water sports activities, and children's clubs, ensuring that every member of the family has something to enjoy.
- **Exceptional Service:** Above all, what sets luxury resorts in Ksamil apart is their commitment to providing exceptional service and personalized attention to guests. From the minute you arrive until you leave, our committed team strives to anticipate and surpass your every need, delivering a genuinely exceptional experience.

Budget-Friendly Hotels

When planning a vacation to Ksamil, choose budget-friendly hotels for practical and pleasant lodgings without breaking the bank. These hotels provide guests with a convenient base from which to explore Ksamil's gorgeous beaches, historical monuments, and cultural activities while staying within budget. In this part, we'll look at the characteristics and benefits of low-cost hotels in Ksamil to help you locate the ideal location to stay without sacrificing quality.

- **Affordable Rates:** Budget-friendly hotels in Ksamil are recognized for their low prices, making them an

appealing alternative for budget-conscious guests. Whether you're traveling alone, with family, or in a group, these hotels provide value without compromising comfort or convenience.
- **Central Locations:** Many inexpensive hotels in Ksamil are conveniently positioned near the town center, beaches, and major attractions. This excellent location enables visitors to explore the surrounding region on foot, reducing transportation expenses and increasing time spent enjoying the sights and sounds of Ksamil.
- **Comfortable Accommodations:** While budget-friendly hotels may have fewer frills than luxury hotels, they still have clean, comfortable rooms with important facilities like comfy mattresses, en-suite bathrooms, air conditioning, and Wi-Fi. Guests may anticipate a comfortable and inviting environment that seems like a home away from home.
- **Pleasant Service:** Despite their low prices, Ksamil hotels take pleasure in delivering pleasant and attentive service to their visitors. From check-in to check-out, hotel personnel are dedicated to delivering a comfortable and hassle-free stay by assisting with baggage, arranging transportation, and recommending area meals and activities.
- **Complimentary Breakfast**: Many low-cost hotels in Ksamil include complimentary breakfast as part of the accommodation tariff, allowing customers to start their

day with a substantial meal before venturing out. To fuel your activities, we provide a variety of continental and traditional Albanian cuisine, as well as freshly prepared coffee and refreshing juice.

- **Additional facilities**: While facilities vary per hotel, low-cost hotels in Ksamil frequently provide access to common spaces like lounges, terraces, and gardens where visitors may rest and interact. Some hotels may additionally include laundry services, bicycle rentals, and tour booking services to improve the visitor experience.
- **Flexibility:** Most budget-friendly hotels in Ksamil have flexible booking choices, enabling customers to select from a variety of accommodation types and durations to fit their trip requirements. These hotels cater to a variety of requirements and interests, whether you're staying for one night or several days.
- **Local Insights:** One of the benefits of staying in low-cost hotels is the ability to meet with locals who may give helpful tips and recommendations for seeing Ksamil and its surroundings. From secret beaches and hiking trails to unique eateries and cultural events, hotel staff can help you explore the finest of Ksamil without breaking the budget.

Overall, budget-friendly hotels in Ksamil are an excellent option for tourists looking for economical lodging without sacrificing quality or convenience. With their central locations, pleasant accommodations, courteous service, and cheap pricing, these hotels are ideal for exploring Ksamil's beauty and charm on a budget.

Boutique Guesthouses

Boutique guesthouses in Ksamil are an appealing alternative to standard hotels for guests looking for a more intimate and personalized overnight experience. These small-scale lodgings blend distinctive architecture, kind hospitality, and meticulous attention to detail to create a one-of-a-kind ambiance that embodies Ksamil's personality and culture. In this part, we delve into the attraction of boutique guesthouses, encouraging you to discover the hidden treasures of Ksamil's hospitality sector.

- **Intimate Atmosphere:** Unlike larger hotels, boutique guesthouses in Ksamil offer a cozy and intimate atmosphere that fosters genuine connections between guests and hosts. With fewer rooms and a focus on customized service, visitors can anticipate a warm greeting and personalized care during their stay.
- **Unique Design:** Boutique guesthouses are well-known for their distinct design and character, which frequently reflect Ksamil's architecture, culture, and aesthetics. From lovely stone facades and colorful interiors to handcrafted furniture and handmade décor,

each guesthouse has its narrative and welcomes tourists to immerse themselves in the destination's beauty and charm.

- **Individual Service:** One of the distinguishing features of boutique guesthouses is their focus on individual service and hospitality. Owners and staff go above and above to make visitors feel welcome, cherished, and cared for throughout their stay, providing insider information, fulfilling special requests, and creating unforgettable experiences.
- **Authentic Experiences**: Staying at a boutique guesthouse allows visitors to discover the true spirit of Ksamil, away from the throngs and commercialism of larger hotels. Engage in meaningful conversations with hosts and fellow guests, participate in cultural activities and customs, and enjoy home-cooked meals produced with love and care from locally sourced ingredients.
- **Attention to Detail:** Boutique guesthouses thrill visitors with thoughtful touches and attention to detail that boost the whole experience from the moment they enter. Whether it's fresh flowers in your room, homemade toiletries, or nightly turndown service, every part of your stay is intended to surpass your expectations and create lasting memories.
- **Exclusive facilities:** Boutique guesthouses, despite their modest size, provide a variety of facilities and

services to improve the visitor experience. Enjoy complimentary breakfast with handcrafted pastries and organic vegetables, unwind in pleasant lounges or gardens, and use concierge services to book activities, excursions, and dining reservations.

- **Peace & Tranquility:** Boutique guesthouses frequently have beautiful and isolated surroundings, offering visitors a peaceful respite from the rush and bustle of everyday life. Whether set among beautiful gardens, overlooking the sea, or tucked away in a quaint hamlet, these guesthouses provide a haven for travelers to relax, rejuvenate, and reconnect with nature and themselves.
- **Community Connection:** Choosing to stay in a boutique guesthouse helps the local economy and community by supporting small businesses and promoting sustainable tourist practices. Many guesthouses work with local artists, farmers, and producers to encourage cultural preservation and environmental sustainability, allowing visitors to form meaningful relationships with their location.

In a nutshell, the boutique guesthouses in Ksamil provide a totally original and immersive accommodation experience, combining customized service, distinctive decor, and genuine hospitality to create amazing moments. Whether you're looking for a romantic trip, a calm retreat, or a cultural adventure, boutique guesthouses allow you to immerse yourself in Ksamil's heart and soul in a way that's as distinctive and unforgettable as the place.

Unique Stays

Ksamil, with its stunning scenery and rich cultural past, has a wealth of unique lodgings that guarantee remarkable experiences for guests looking for something out of the usual. From eco-friendly lodges secluded in nature to ancient villas steeped in charm, these one-of-a-kind lodgings give a magical touch to your Ksamil experience.

- **Eco-Friendly Retreats:** Immerse yourself in nature and sustainability at one of Ksamil's eco-friendly retreats. These eco-friendly lodgings stress environmental protection and allow guests to reconnect with nature. Stay at eco-friendly bungalows or treehouses set among lush woods, participate in organic agricultural activities, and learn about sustainable living techniques throughout your stay.
- **Historical Villas and Estates**: Step back in time and experience the grandeur of bygone eras at one of Ksamil's historical villas and estates. These painstakingly restored buildings provide a view into the region's rich history and architectural magnificence, with magnificent furniture, extravagant décor, and extensive gardens that exude timeless

elegance and refinement. Indulge in luxury and refinement while learning about Ksamil's rich history and culture.
- **Secluded Beach Cabins:** For those seeking peace and tranquility, secluded beach cabins are the ideal getaway from the rush and bustle of everyday life. Nestled along the coast, these beautiful cabins provide unobstructed views of the sea and direct access to pristine beaches, allowing visitors to relax and recharge in a peaceful and ideal location. Take a stroll along the beach, stargaze beneath the night sky, and fall asleep to the calm sound of waves lapping against the coast.
- **Floating Bungalows:** Staying in a floating home offers the finest in lakeside life. These one-of-a-kind bungalows sit atop the peaceful waters of Ksamil's lagoons, providing panoramic views of the surrounding environment. Wake up to the sight of sun-dappled seas and vibrant marine life, dine alfresco on your private terrace, and relax in the tranquility of your aquatic refuge.
- **Cave Dwellings:** Immerse yourself in history by staying in a cave residence, where modern amenities blend with prehistoric elegance. Carved within the craggy cliffs of Ksamil, these cave rooms provide a totally unique hotel experience, complete with natural rock formations, comfortable interiors, and panoramic sea views. Discover the fascination of cave-

dwelling while exploring the natural beauty of Ksamil's coastline and uncovering the mysteries concealed inside its rocky landscape.
- **Treehouse Retreats:** Enhance your Ksamil experience by staying in a treehouse hideaway, where childhood aspirations meet adult luxury. Perched high amid the woods, these beautiful apartments exude whimsy and enchantment, with rustic charm and modern comforts suitable for tourists of all ages. Spend your days exploring the surrounding forest, seeing wildlife, and bonding with nature in this absolutely lovely environment.
- **Glamping Sites:** A stay at a premium glamping site offers the best of both worlds, combining outdoor adventure with posh comfort. These opulent camping accommodations provide attractive tents, comfy furniture, and private conveniences, allowing visitors to appreciate nature's grandeur without giving up the comforts of home. Whether you're eating marshmallows over the campfire or stargazing from your comfortable bed, glamping in Ksamil provides an unforgettable outdoor experience.
- **Underwater Hotels:** Immerse yourself in a world of wonder by staying in an underwater hotel, where visitors may sleep under the waters and witness the beauty of the underwater environment firsthand. These revolutionary lodgings have glass walls and

ceilings, providing unmatched views of the aquatic life that surrounds you. Immerse yourself in the peacefulness of the ocean, marvel at the colorful coral reefs, and see the beauty of Ksamil's underwater ecology from the comfort of your magnificent room.

From eco-friendly getaways to underwater hotels, Ksamil's unique stays provide an unprecedented chance to engage with nature, history, and culture in ways that are both memorable and spectacular.

Top Recommended Accommodation

Choosing the right lodging is critical while organizing your trip to Ksamil. With so many alternatives available, it might be difficult to decide where to stay. To help you make an informed selection, we've compiled a list of the best Ksamil lodgings, each of which provides great service, comfort, and value to travelers of all tastes and budgets.

- **Hotel Riviera:** Located only steps from Ksamil's gorgeous beaches, Hotel Riviera embodies elegance and tranquillity. This seaside hideaway offers spacious accommodations, modern conveniences, and panoramic views of the Ionian Sea, making it the ideal of comfort and convenience for travelers visiting Ksamil.

- **Villa Ksamil:** Nestled among green gardens and olive groves, Villa Ksamil exudes charm and sophistication. This boutique hotel, owned by a kind family, radiates both warmth and refinement. Villa Ksamil welcomes guests with cozy rooms, individualized service, and a tranquil setting, providing a sanctuary-like experience.
- **EcoLodge Ksamil:** Catering to environmentally aware guests, EcoLodge Ksamil provides a unique and sustainable hotel option. Nestled in the Albanian countryside, this eco-retreat offers cozy accommodations, organic cuisine, and ecologically aware services, allowing guests to relax and rejuvenate while reducing their environmental imprint.
- **Seaside Bungalows:** Escape the city noise and experience seaside quiet at Seaside Bungalows, where rustic charm meets beachside tranquillity. Perched amid the tranquil waters of Lake Ksamil, these cozy bungalows provide visitors with a quiet getaway surrounded by nature's embrace. Wake up to the rhythmic music of waves, explore surrounding beaches and attractions, and enjoy the comfort of your quiet hideaway.
- **Villa Bella:** Radiating Ksamil's laid-back charm, Villa Bella welcomes guests of all ages with open arms. This family-friendly retreat provides comfortable rooms,

child-friendly facilities, and attentive service, creating a peaceful and familial setting in which cherished memories are formed.
- **The Beach House:** Experience true coastal life at The Beach House, a boutique hotel overlooking the Ionian Sea's cerulean seas. With its trendy decor, coastal location, and personalized service, The Beach House provides visitors with an exceptional seaside getaway in the heart of Ksamil.
- **Ksamil Sunset Resort:** Ksamil Sunset Resort combines sophistication and tranquillity to create grandeur. Perched on a hill above Ksamil town, this upmarket resort offers spectacular views, opulent suites, and world-class services, resulting in an unrivaled indulgent retreat for discriminating tourists.
- **Villa Paradise:** Discover a hidden refuge at Villa Paradise, a charming bed and breakfast tucked in Ksamil's picturesque countryside. Villa Paradise, with its cozy rooms, lush gardens, and friendly service, provides visitors with a tranquil escape from the city, encouraging them to rest and revitalize surrounded by nature.

In a nutshell, the best-suggested lodgings in Ksamil embody the spirit of hospitality, combining comfort, convenience, and charm to offer a wonderful stay.

Choosing the Right Accommodation for You

Choosing the right lodging is an important part of any trip planning since it has a huge impact on the whole experience. Ksamil, a beachfront treasure located along the Albanian Riviera, has a variety of hotel alternatives that may be both thrilling and intimidating.

In this part, we'll go over the key things to consider when selecting the best lodging for your needs, guaranteeing a memorable and pleasurable stay in Ksamil.

- **Budget:** Determine your range of hotel expenditures. Ksamil has a wide range of housing options, from budget-friendly guesthouses to luxury resorts, allowing guests with varying budgets to choose acceptable lodgings without sacrificing comfort or convenience.
- **Location:** Think about where you want to stay in respect to your planned activities and Ksamil attractions. Choose a location that fits your interests and schedule, whether it's a beachside hideaway, a peaceful countryside escape, or a central position among restaurants and activities.
- **Accommodation Type:** Identify the type of accommodation that best suits your travel style and

preferences. Whether you prefer the personalized care of a boutique guesthouse, the comforts of a luxury resort, the elegance of a historic villa, or the flexibility of a rental apartment, select the type of accommodation that best suits your needs.
- **Amenities and Facilities:** Consider the amenities and facilities provided by the hotel, such as Wi-Fi, air conditioning, complimentary breakfast, swimming pools, spa services, and recreational activities. Prioritize things that are necessary for your comfort and enjoyment throughout your stay in Ksamil.
- **Reviews and Ratings:** Look up reviews and ratings from past guests to determine the quality and reputation of the hotel. Websites and platforms like TripAdvisor, Booking.com, and Airbnb give useful information and comments from visitors who have stayed at the hotel, allowing you to make an informed selection.
- **Accessibility:** Assess the accommodation's accessibility in terms of transit alternatives, parking availability, and closeness to public transportation hubs. Choose hotels with easy access to neighboring attractions, beaches, restaurants, and shopping centers, which will make your stay more comfortable and enjoyable.
- **Cancellation Policy:** Learn about the accommodations' cancellation policy and reservation

restrictions. Choose hotels with flexible cancellation policies, which allow for adjustments or cancellations without incurring significant fines, offering peace of mind and flexibility in the event of unanticipated situations.

- **Special Requirements:** If you have any specific requirements or preferences, such as pet-friendly accommodations, wheelchair accessibility, dietary restrictions, or family-friendly amenities, please communicate them to the accommodation provider ahead of time to ensure a smooth and comfortable stay.
- **Authenticity & Local Experience**: Look for lodgings that provide an authentic and immersive experience of Ksamil culture, tradition, and hospitality. Prioritize lodgings that enable you to engage with the local community and culture, whether it means staying in a traditional guesthouse owned by a local family, engaging in cultural events and seminars, or enjoying true Albanian food.
- **Personal Preferences:** When it comes to picking the best lodging for your vacation to Ksamil, trust your instincts and preferences. Consider ambiance, mood, and general vibe that align with your interests and preferences to ensure a memorable and gratifying experience that represents your distinct travel style.

By taking these important criteria into account and analyzing your objectives and interests, you can select the ideal lodging to improve your experience and create lasting memories during your vacation to Ksamil.

Booking Tips and Tricks

Booking the appropriate lodging in Ksamil takes considerable research and strategic preparation. Here are some important tips and strategies to assist you navigate the booking process and get the greatest selections for your stay:

- **Start Early:** Plan your hotel search well in advance of your trip dates, especially if you want to visit during high seasons or holidays. Early booking boosts your chances of discovering available rooms and allows you to benefit from early bird discounts and specials.
- **Set a Budget:** Determine and stick to your lodging budget. Consider hotel prices, extra fees, and taxes when estimating the overall cost of your stay in Ksamil. Be cautious of your financial restrictions to prevent splurging on lodging fees.
- **Research Thoroughly:** Explore a variety of accommodation options in Ksamil, including hotels, guesthouses, rental apartments, and resorts. Read reviews, look at photographs, and compare amenities to discover the perfect option for your interests and travel style.

- **Consider Location:** Select an accommodation that is close to the sites and activities you intend to enjoy in Ksamil. Whether you choose a beachside setting, a central urban district, or a peaceful countryside getaway, select lodgings that fit your schedule and preferences.
- **Date Flexibility:** To take advantage of lower prices and special deals, keep your trip dates flexible. Consider moving your arrival and departure dates a few days apart to take advantage of off-peak prices and availability.
- **Look for Deals and Discounts:** Keep an eye out for special bargains, discounts, and package deals offered by booking websites, travel agencies, and lodging providers. Subscribe to newsletters and follow social media profiles to remain informed about limited-time deals and flash sales.
- **Book Directly:** Consider booking directly with the lodging provider to receive special discounts and advantages that are not available through third-party booking systems. Direct booking also provides for improved communication and flexibility in the event of modifications or specific requirements.
- **Check Cancellation Policies:** Before booking a reservation, review possible lodgings' cancellation policies. Choose lodgings with flexible cancellation policies, which provide full or partial refunds in the

event of unforeseen changes to your vacation arrangements.
- **Utilize Reward Programs:** Take advantage of loyalty programs and reward systems provided by hotels and booking sites to earn points, discounts, and complimentary upgrades. Joining loyalty programs might result in substantial discounts and other rewards during your stay in Ksamil.
- **Read the Fine Print:** Carefully consider your reservation's terms and conditions, including payment options, check-in/out timings, and any additional fees or charges. Pay close attention to any limits or conditions set by the accommodation to prevent confusion or surprises upon arrival.

By using these booking tips and techniques, you may simplify the hotel-choosing process and acquire the perfect accommodations for your unforgettable trip to Ksamil.

Chapter 4

EXPLORING KSAMIL

Ksamil, located on the gorgeous Albanian Riviera, is a refuge for vacationers seeking sun-kissed beaches, unspoiled landscapes, and unrivaled natural beauty.

In this chapter, we will take a journey to discover the mesmerizing views and attractions that make Ksamil a must-see destination for nature lovers, beachgoers, and adventurers alike.

Beaches and Coastline

Ksamil is known for its beautiful beaches and crystal-clear seas, making it a popular destination for sunbathers and water enthusiasts. Here are some of the best beaches and coastal attractions to visit:

- **Ksamil Beach:** Ksamil Beach, the crown gem of Ksamil, captivates visitors with its smooth white beaches and blue waves. This lovely beach, surrounded by green hills and waving palm trees, provides many

chances for swimming, sunbathing, and snorkeling in stunning coastal landscapes.
- **Pasqyra Beach:** Tucked away from the masses, Pasqyra Beach offers a serene shoreline and clean waves, making it ideal for anyone seeking a peaceful retreat. Surrounded by cliffs and thick flora, this quiet beach provides a peaceful escape for nature enthusiasts and those seeking seclusion.
- **Mirrors Beach**: Named after its mirrored seas and mirror-like surface, Mirrors Beach captivates tourists with its surreal beauty and untouched environment. Nestled in a quiet cove, this hidden gem provides a private retreat for swimming, kayaking, and enjoying nature's peace.
- **Xhami Beach:** With its shallow waves and family-friendly ambiance, Xhami Beach is a popular location for families with children. The mild waves and smooth beaches make it a great location for swimming, sandcastle building, and picnics with loved ones while enjoying panoramic sea views.
- **Ferhati Beach**: Surrounded by thick flora and rocky outcrops, Ferhati Beach invites explorers and nature lovers to discover its raw beauty. With its pure seas and impressive shoreline, this secret beach is ideal for snorkeling, rock climbing, and exploring hidden coves and caves along the shore.

- **Pulebardha Beach:** Known as "Seagull Beach," Pulebardha Beach is a peaceful refuge hidden along the Ksamil coast. This picturesque beach, known for its tranquil waves and golden beaches, provides a serene escape for sunbathing, swimming, and watching the sunset against a backdrop of flying seagulls and azure sky.
- **Lekursi Castle Beach:** Located underneath the old Lekursi Castle, Lekursi Castle Beach provides panoramic views of the Ionian Sea and the surrounding environment. This quiet beach, accessible by a picturesque footpath or boat ride, offers a tranquil location for swimming, snorkeling, and discovering the underwater treasures of Ksamil's coastal ecology.
- **Sunset Beach**: Sunset Beach, called after its magnificent sunsets, captivates visitors with its golden beaches and brilliant colors splashed across the sky. Located on Ksamil's western shore, this lovely beach provides a romantic location for evening strolls, seaside eating, and capturing unforgettable moments against the backdrop of the sunset.

From secluded coves to sun-kissed coastlines, Ksamil's beaches and coastline beckon visitors to immerse themselves in the natural magnificence and coastal charm of this wonderful location.

Natural Attractions.

In addition to its beautiful beaches, Ksamil has a wide range of natural attractions that highlight the region's biological richness and visual attractiveness. Here are some must-see natural sights in Kasamil:

- **Butrint National Park:** A UNESCO World Heritage Site, Butrint National Park contains a wealth of archaeological treasures and natural landscapes. This large park, which includes ancient ruins, natural marshes, and deep woods, is ideal for trekking, birding, and discovering the region's rich cultural legacy.
- **Blue Eye Spring**: Tucked away in the heart of the Albanian countryside, the Blue Eye Spring is a natural wonder known for its bright blue waters and magical depth. This exquisite spring, fed by subterranean streams and surrounded by thick flora, allows visitors to marvel at its beauty while immersing themselves in nature's peacefulness.
- **Syri i Kalter:** Translated as "The Blue Eye," Syri i Kalter is a natural spring that enchants visitors with its crystalline waters and fascinating colors of blue. Nestled among green landscapes and limestone cliffs, this hidden gem provides a tranquil location for leisure, photography, and exploration of the surrounding countryside.

- **Ksamil Islands**: Take a boat excursion to the Ksamil Islands, a collection of lovely islands spread across the Ionian Sea. With their beautiful beaches, quiet coves, and diverse marine life, these islands are a haven for snorkelers, kayakers, and beachcombers seeking adventure and discovery.
- **Borsh Waterfall:** Located near the town of Borsh, Borsh Waterfall is a magnificent waterfall that cascades down the slope, creating a natural sight between lush trees and jagged rocks. Visitors may climb to the waterfall's base, swim in the calm waters, and have a picnic in the serene surroundings.
- **Llogara Pass**: Climb to the picturesque heights of Llogara Pass, a hilly route that runs through the Llogara National Park. This beautiful vantage point, which provides panoramic views of the Ionian shoreline and Albanian Riviera, is a favorite destination for photographers, hikers, and nature lovers looking for panoramic panoramas and pure mountain air.
- **Gjipe Canyon:** Carved by the Gjipe River, Gjipe Canyon is a natural beauty with towering cliffs, turquoise seas, and unspoiled beaches. This hidden jewel, accessible by boat or hiking route, provides possibilities for swimming, rock climbing, and exploration of Albania's rough coastline landscapes.
- **Ksamil Olive Groves**: Walk through the serene olive groves of Ksamil, where old trees and lush vegetation

form a peaceful sanctuary in the Mediterranean environment. Discover the centuries-old history of olive growing, taste locally made olive oil, and be immersed in the timeless beauty of Ksamil's agricultural legacy.

From flowing waterfalls to hidden springs, Ksamil's natural features urge visitors to immerse themselves in the pristine beauty and biological diversity of this beautiful place.

Parks and Gardens

In addition to its breathtaking coastline and natural beauty, Ksamil has several parks and gardens that highlight the region's biodiversity, vegetation, and wildlife. These natural parks offer peaceful getaways for rest, recreation, and admiration of nature's beauty. Here are some interesting parks and gardens to visit in Ksamil:

- **Ksamil National Park:** Nestled along the Ionian Sea's coastline, Ksamil National Park is a magnificent paradise filled with lush flora, scenic pathways, and different wildlife habitats. Visitors may wander around the park's unspoiled landscapes, picnic in sheltered woods, and enjoy panoramic views of the coastline and adjacent islands. Ksamil National Park, with its well-kept trails and natural features, provides a tranquil location for outdoor activity and nature enjoyment.

- **Ksamil Botanical Gardens:** Enjoy the vivid colors and fragrant blossoms of Ksamil Botanical Gardens, a beautiful oasis in the center of the hamlet. The botanical gardens, which feature a broad assortment of local and exotic plant species such as floral shrubs, towering trees, and scented herbs, are a sensory feast for both nature lovers and gardening enthusiasts. Visitors may walk along meandering walkways, see seasonal displays, and learn about the region's rich botanical heritage via informative signs and guided tours.
- **Lekursi Castle Gardens:** Located on a picturesque hill above Ksamil, Lekursi Castle Gardens provides panoramic views of the surrounding environment and shoreline. Visitors may tour the castle's medieval grounds, stroll through groomed gardens, and enjoy panoramic views of the Ionian Sea and distant mountains. Lekursi Castle Gardens, with its tranquil environment and breathtaking splendor, offers a peaceful escape for quiet thought, romantic strolls, and wonderful picture possibilities.
- **Vivari Channel Park:** Nestled on the Vivari Channel, this delightful park is a hidden gem where lush flora meets peaceful waters. Visitors may rest along shaded walks, enjoy magnificent views of the channel, and witness a variety of bird species that live in the wetland habitat. Vivari Channel Park's serene environment and

natural attractiveness make it a popular site for birding, photography, and leisurely picnics by the water.
- **Ksamil Olive Grove:** Take a tour through Ksamil's historic olive groves, where centuries-old trees serve as living testaments to the region's agricultural legacy. Visitors may stroll through sun-dappled orchards, learn about traditional olive farming techniques, and sample locally made olive oil at surrounding farms and presses. With its quiet ambiance and timeless beauty, the olive grove provides a peaceful respite from the rush and bustle of contemporary life, encouraging guests to reconnect with nature and enjoy the simple joys of country living.
- **Ksamil Coastal Promenade:** The Ksamil Coastal Promenade is a magnificent promenade that runs along the coastline, providing stunning views of the sea, sandy beaches, and distant islands. Visitors may stroll down the promenade, enjoy the fresh sea breezes, and take in the beauty of Ksamil's coastal scenery. With its attractive cafés, modest shops, and dynamic ambiance, the promenade is a favorite gathering spot for both residents and tourists, providing a delightful combination of coastal charm and Mediterranean warmth.
- **Ksamil Butterfly Park:** Explore the magical world of butterflies at Ksamil Butterfly Park, a peaceful haven

where multicolored butterflies glide among lush vegetation and brilliant flowers. Visitors may stroll through themed gardens, witness butterfly species from all around the world, and learn about the delicate balance of ecosystems that sustain these exquisite insects. Ksamil Butterfly Park, with its serene environment and natural beauty, offers a unique opportunity to interact with nature while marveling at the wonders of the insect world.

Ksamil's green areas, which range from stunning parks to botanical gardens, provide a calm getaway for tourists to immerse themselves in nature's beauty and enjoy the healing power of the great outdoors.

Chapter 5

CUISINE AND DINING

Ksamil's food scene exemplifies Albania's rich cultural past, combining traditional tastes, fresh ingredients, and culinary artistry.

In this chapter, we look at the many meals, seafood specialties, and dining experiences that Ksamil has to offer visitors.

Traditional Albanian Dishes

Albanian cuisine is known for its simplicity, freshness, and concentration on locally obtained ingredients. Albanian cuisine draws inspiration from Mediterranean and Balkan culinary traditions, resulting in a harmonious combination of tastes and textures that appeal to the senses. Here are some classic Albanian foods to try in Ksamil:

- **Tave Kosi:** A popular Albanian dish, Tave Kosi is a substantial casserole cooked with soft lamb or beef, yogurt, and eggs, seasoned with garlic, mint, and olive

oil. The dish is cooked to perfection until the yogurt produces a golden crust, resulting in a creamy texture and savory taste that pleases the palette.
- **Fërgesë:** A tasty stew cooked with roasted peppers, tomatoes, onions, and meats like veal, chicken, or sausage. The recipe is carefully cooked to enable the flavors to combine, producing a rich and cozy supper that is frequently eaten with crusty bread or rice.
- **Byrek**: Byrek is a traditional Albanian pastry made of layers of thin phyllo dough with a savory filling like spinach, cheese, or minced beef. The pastry is cooked until golden and crispy, resulting in a delicious combination of textures and aromas that is ideal for snacking or a light dinner.
- **Qofte:** Qofte is a typical Albanian meatball made with minced beef, onions, herbs, and spices, which are formed into tiny patties and cooked till golden brown. These savory meatballs are generally served with rice, salad, or tangy tomato sauce, making them a popular comfort dish among Albanian families.
- **Fërgesë of Tirana:** This regional variant of the original fërgesë combines roasted peppers, tomatoes, and onions with pieces of delicate lamb or beef. The dish is seasoned with a variety of fragrant herbs and spices, resulting in a hearty and delicious dinner that is popular across Albania.

- **Tavë Dheu:** This rustic meal, also known as "Mountain Casserole," highlights the tastes of Albania's rough surroundings. Tavë Dheu is a rich and comfortable dinner made with meats, potatoes, and vegetables, slow-cooked to perfection. It's ideal for winter evenings.
- **Bakllavë:** Bakllavë is a popular Albanian dessert that complements any meal. This delectable pastry is constructed with layers of thin phyllo dough, butter, and chopped nuts steeped in a fragrant syrup of honey, sugar, and spices. Bakllavë is traditionally served at important events and festivals, representing hospitality and festivity in Albanian culture.
- **Fli:** Fli is a classic Albanian delicacy created with layers of thin pancake-like crepes alternating with a creamy filling of eggs, milk, and sugar. The dish is cooked till golden and crispy, then drizzled with honey and topped with cinnamon, resulting in a sweet and rich delicacy ideal for sharing with loved ones.

From savory stews to indulgent pastries, traditional Albanian dishes offer a tantalizing glimpse into the culinary heritage and cultural traditions of Ksamil and its people.

Local Seafood Specialties

Ksamil, a seaside town, has a thriving culinary scene, with seafood taking center stage. Fresh catches from the Ionian Sea inspire a wide range of delectable meals that reflect the area's marine wealth. Here are some local seafood dishes to try in Ksamil:

- **Grilled Sea Bass:** Fresh sea bass from local waterways is seasoned with aromatic herbs, olive oil, and a touch of lemon before masterfully grilling to perfection. The end product is a delicious meal that embodies the spirit of Mediterranean cuisine.
- **Stuffed Squid:** Soft squid tubes are stuffed with a delicious mixture of breadcrumbs, herbs, garlic, and spices and gently cooked in a rich tomato sauce until soft. Stuffed squid exemplifies the expert combination of tastes and textures that characterizes Albanian seafood cuisine.
- **Seafood Pasta:** Al dente pasta is mixed with a mixture of fresh seafood, including shrimp, mussels, and clams, in a delicious tomato-based sauce flavored with garlic, pepper flakes, and parsley. Seafood pasta is a warm and fulfilling dish that honors the ocean's abundance with each bite.
- **Grilled Octopus:** Soft octopus tentacles are marinated in olive oil, garlic, and lemon juice before grilling over

an open flame until charred and soft. Grilled octopus is a traditional Mediterranean treat that goes well with crisp salads and cold white wine.
- **Seafood Risotto:** The combination of big shrimp, soft calamari, and sweet scallops adds a sea taste to this creamy risotto. Finished with a sprinkling of Parmesan cheese and fresh herbs, seafood risotto is a sumptuous and decadent dish that delights the palate.
- **Fried Anchovies:** Fresh anchovies are coated in seasoned flour, and then fried until golden and crispy. Fried anchovies, served with a splash of lemon and tartar sauce, are a favorite appetizer or snack among both residents and visitors.
- **Seafood Platter:** For a delicious feast, serve grilled fish, shrimp, calamari, and shellfish with a variety of dipping sauces and freshly baked bread. A seafood platter is ideal for sharing and tasting the full range of tastes that Ksamil's seaside cuisine has to provide.
- **Squid Ink Risotto:** Creamy risotto imbued with the saline aroma of squid ink is garnished with soft squid, resulting in a visually remarkable and savory meal that is as rewarding to eat as it is attractive to look at.

Ksamil's seafood specialties range from grilled delicacies to delicious pasta dishes, demonstrating the region's culinary ability and profound connection to the sea.

Dining Etiquette & Tips

To properly enjoy the gastronomic wonders of Ksamil, it is vital to follow local dining etiquette and customs. Here are some suggestions for having a memorable and delightful eating experience in Ksamil:

- **Respect Local Customs:** Learn about Albanian eating customs and traditions, such as greeting others before meals and expressing thanks afterward. Respect for local customs promotes goodwill and improves your eating experience in Ksamil.
- **Make Reservations:** To ensure a table and avoid long wait times at popular restaurants and eating venues, make reservations ahead of time, especially during busy tourist seasons. For added convenience, several Ksamil restaurants accept online reservations.
- **Dress Appropriately:** Although Ksamil has a relaxed and casual attitude, it is traditional to dress modestly when dining out, particularly in luxury restaurants or formal settings. When dining in restaurants, avoid beach wear and instead dress neatly and presentably.
- **Tipping Etiquette:** Tipping in Albania is appreciated but not required. If you receive great service, it is usual to tip 5-10% of the entire amount. Tipping is usually done in cash and handed straight to the server or left on the table at the end of the dinner.

- **Sample Local Specialties:** Take advantage of the chance to learn about Albanian cuisine by experiencing local specialties and regional delicacies. When sampling new meals, be adventurous and open-minded. Don't be afraid to ask your waitress for recommendations or explanations of unusual menu items.
- **Enjoy Leisurely Meals:** Dining in Ksamil is a relaxing experience, with dinners frequently lasting several hours as guests appreciate each course and participate in spirited discussions. Accept the casual pace of dinner and take the time to savor the flavors, fragrances, and conversation of your companions.
- **Be Aware of Dietary Restrictions:** If you have any dietary restrictions or food allergies, explain these to your server when making your order. Many restaurants in Ksamil are used to accommodating dietary restrictions and can provide acceptable alternatives or menu changes.
- **Indulge in Local Produce:** Ksamil is recognized for its fresh fish, locally produced produce, and handcrafted products. Take advantage of the wealth of seasonal fruits, vegetables, and seafood available, and experience the region's tastes with each meal.

By adhering to dining etiquette and adopting Ksamil culinary customs, you may fully immerse yourself in local culture and have a great dining experience that honors Albania's rich tastes and warmth.

Chapter 6

SHOPPING AND MARKETS

Ksamil has a thriving retail scene where visitors may immerse themselves in the local culture, peruse unusual goods, and tour crowded marketplaces.

This chapter explores the varied shopping experiences available to guests in Ksamil, ranging from traditional trinkets to sophisticated retail centers.

Souvenirs and Handicrafts

Exploring Ksamil's souvenir stores and craft boutiques is an important element of the trip experience. Whether you're looking for traditional memories or one-of-a-kind treasures, Ksamil's artisan community has a wide selection of handcrafted crafts and souvenirs that encapsulate the essence of Albanian culture. Here are some popular souvenirs and handicrafts to explore:

- **Handmade Textiles**: Discover Ksamil's rich textile legacy via handmade carpets, tapestries, and

traditional costumes created by local artists. These exquisite fabrics highlight Albania's cultural richness and creative mastery, making them valuable keepsakes for tourists looking for original gifts.
- **Ceramics and Pottery:** Visit Ksamil's pottery studios and workshops to see a colorful collection of handcrafted ceramics, including plates, bowls, vases, and ornamental tiles embellished with traditional themes and designs. Each work shows the expertise and creativity of local artists, providing a concrete memento of your stay in Ksamil.
- **Embroidered Textiles:** Admire Ksamil's amazing embroidery and craftsmanship, which includes tablecloths, pillow coverings, and traditional clothes with vibrant designs and themes. These carefully woven textiles reflect Albania's rich cultural past and are highly valued for their beauty and craftsmanship.
- **Woodcarvings:** Explore the creativity of Albanian woodcarvers via elaborately carved figures, jewelry boxes, and ornamental objects made of locally obtained wood. Ksamil's woodcarvings range from delicate filigree motifs to strong geometric patterns, demonstrating the artisan community's ability and originality.
- **Olive Wood objects:** Celebrate Albania's olive-growing legacy with handcrafted olive wood objects such as cutting boards, household utensils, and

decorative elements. Olive wood's unusual texture and durability make it a popular material for handmade products, offering tourists unique and environmentally friendly keepsakes to appreciate.
- **Traditional Instruments:** Immerse yourself in Albania's musical legacy by playing traditional instruments like the çifteli (string instrument), lahuta (lute), and def (frame drum), which are created by experienced artisans using time-honored traditions. Whether you're a music lover or a collector, these original instruments provide a musical reminder of Albanian culture and heritage.
- **Leather products**: Visit Ksamil's leather workshops and stores to find a wide variety of leather products, including purses, belts, shoes, and accessories made from high-quality leather acquired from local tanneries. Each piece exemplifies the quality and attention to detail that distinguish Albanian leatherwork, making it a fashionable and useful keepsake to carry home.
- **Local Artwork:** Support Ksamil's blossoming art scene by visiting galleries and studios that display local artists' paintings, sculptures, and mixed-media artwork. From classic landscapes to modern abstractions, Ksamil's art scene encompasses a wide range of styles and materials that represent the region's cultural legacy and artistic expression.

Exploring Ksamil's handmade stores and souvenir markets allows visitors to engage with local culture, support small companies, and take home significant keepsakes that remind them of their stay in this lovely place.

Local Markets and Bazars

Ksamil's local markets and bazaars are thriving hubs of trade and cultural interaction, where the essence of daily life unfolds against a backdrop of colors, fragrances, and noises. These markets provide a glimpse into the community's heart and soul, highlighting the land's wealth and its residents' inventiveness. Here are some of the busy marketplaces and bazaars to visit in Ksamil.

- **Ksamil Farmer's Market**: Located in the middle of the town, the Ksamil Farmer's Market is a bustling hub of activity where local farmers, artists, and merchants come to sell their products. Visitors may walk through rows of stalls selling fresh fruits, vegetables, herbs, cheeses, honey, and handmade preserves grown in the region's rich fields and orchards. The market provides a sensory experience, with brilliant colors, aromatic fragrances, and lively talk of merchants and buyers generating a sense of community and conviviality.
- **Lekursi Castle Craft Market:** Perched atop a picturesque hill overlooking Ksamil, the Lekursi Castle

Craft Market combines history, culture, and craftsmanship. Set against the backdrop of historic stone walls and panoramic views of the coastline, the market sells a diverse range of handcrafted items, including traditional textiles, pottery, jewelry, leatherwork, and artwork created by local craftsmen. Visitors may browse the stalls, chat with craftsmen, and buy one-of-a-kind gifts reflecting the legacy and ingenuity of Ksamil's artisan community.

- **Ksamil Fish Market:** Located near the port, the Ksamil Fish Market is a thriving hub of seafood business, with fishermen unloading their daily catches and eager customers flocking to acquire the freshest seafood available. The market provides various marine delights drawn straight from the Ionian Sea, including glittering silverfish, plump shrimp, and savory crabs. Visitors may enjoy the vibrant spectacle of auctioneers, barterers, and seafood enthusiasts bargaining over prices and picking the best specimens for their meals.
- **Weekly Bazaars**: Throughout the week, several areas in Ksamil organize weekly bazaars and street markets where sellers congregate to offer a variety of commodities including apparel, shoes, accessories, household items, electronics, and souvenirs. These busy bazaars are a treasure mine of discounts and curiosities, with sellers displaying their items amid a flurry of bustle and excitement. Visitors may peruse the

booths, haggle with merchants, and soak up the bustling atmosphere of these dynamic marketplaces, where the pulse of Ksamil's economic life is strong.

From the vivid colors of the produce market to the delicate workmanship of the artisan booths, Ksamil's markets and bazaars provide a fascinating view into the everyday rhythms and rich tapestry of life in this charming seaside town.

Shopping Districts

Ksamil is home to a variety of shopping areas and retail enclaves, each with its distinct combination of local charm and commercial activity. From crowded promenades to charming lanes, these districts provide a diverse range of retail experiences to suit every taste or inclination. Here are some of the best retail districts to visit in Ksamil:

- **Rruga Ksamil**: As Ksamil's major commercial street, Rruga Ksamil is a lively road lined with a diverse range of stores, cafés, and boutiques. Visitors may walk down this bustling street and shop a variety of things, including apparel, accessories, handicrafts, and souvenirs. Rruga Ksamil provides a fascinating combination of local flare and modern convenience, with fashionable retail boutiques and charming craft studios.

- **Ksamil Shopping Center**: For those looking for a more convenient shopping experience, the Ksamil Shopping Center is a top choice. This contemporary complex has a varied assortment of businesses, including international brands and local retailers, selling everything from fashion and electronics to home décor and groceries. Visitors may also enjoy food options, entertainment facilities, and leisure activities at the shopping mall, making it a one-stop shop for retail therapy and leisure interests.
- **Old Town Quarter:** Discover Ksamil's rich history and charm by touring the Old Town Quarter. This evocative neighborhood is defined by tiny cobblestone lanes, old houses, and secret courtyards where handmade boutiques, antique shops, and art galleries await discovery. Visitors may browse a carefully chosen assortment of vintage treasures, handcrafted crafts, and locally produced items while immersing themselves in the timeless aura of this historic neighborhood.
- **Beachside Promenade**: Enjoy a leisurely shopping experience on Ksamil's lovely promenade. The promenade is lined with kiosks, stores, and vendors selling a wide variety of beachwear, swimwear, accessories, and beach needs. Visitors may explore colorful displays of sarongs, sunglasses, caps, and souvenirs while admiring panoramic views of the

turquoise sea and sandy beaches. The seaside promenade is a thriving hive of activity where tourists may shop, dine, and relax in a laid-back coastal setting.

- **Artisan Markets and Pop-Up Booths**: Visitors to Ksamil may find artisan markets, flea markets, and pop-up booths that highlight the ingenuity and skill of local craftsmen. These ephemeral venues provide an authentic and immersive shopping experience by showcasing handcrafted items, unique artworks, and unique souvenirs. From handcrafted jewelry to traditional fabrics, artisan marketplaces showcase Ksamil's artisanal legacy and creative energy.
- **Village Markets and Rural Outposts**: Go outside the urban center to discover village markets and rural outposts, where traditional business and community intersect. These markets provide an insight into rural life, with merchants offering fresh vegetables, handcrafted delights, and locally sourced items. Visitors may enjoy the unique cuisine and cultural traditions of rural Albania while also helping local farmers and craftspeople.
- **specialist Stores & Boutiques**: Ksamil is home to several specialist stores and boutiques that cater to certain hobbies and preferences. These places, ranging from gourmet food shops to vintage boutiques, provide carefully curated collections of high-quality items and unique bargains. Visitors may browse specialist stores

selling olive oil, wine, cheese, and other regional delicacies, as well as boutiques featuring handcrafted crafts, designer couture, and artisanal items.

Chapter 7

NIGHTLIFE AND ENTERTAINMENT

Ksamil's nightlife culture is as active as its sunny days, with a diverse range of places and events for guests to enjoy after the sun has set.

This chapter delves into Ksamil's varied range of entertainment options, which include comfortable cafés, pulsing nightclubs, and cultural shows.

Bars and Cafés

Ksamil's pubs and cafés are ideal for mingling, unwinding, and enjoying the local cuisine. Ksamil's pubs and cafés cater to a wide range of tastes and preferences, from a relaxed ambiance for a leisurely drink to a bustling place for a night of dancing. Here are some of the best places to check out:

- **Sunset Lounge:** Perched on the shore, Sunset Lounge provides amazing views of the sunset over the Ionian Sea. It's the perfect place to unwind with a cool drink and take in the panoramic views, thanks to its trendy

design, laid-back atmosphere, and varied cocktail menu. Live music performances and special events enhance the charm of this renowned seaside club.
- **Café del Mar:** Inspired by Ibiza's famed beach club, Café del Mar adds a touch of Mediterranean flair to Ksamil's beaches. This laid-back establishment, located directly on the beach, has comfy seating, ambient music, and a menu of traditional drinks, refreshing smoothies, and light nibbles. Relax on a sunbed with your favorite drink in hand and let the serene atmosphere of Café del Mar wash over you.
- **Tropical Beach Bar:** Surrounded by lush foliage and swaying palm palms, Tropical Beach Bar emanates tropical charm and island feelings. With its colorful design, hammock sitting, and beachside setting, it's the ideal place to drink exotic cocktails, sample fresh fruit juices, and eat great nibbles while basking in the sea wind and sunshine.
- **Moonlight Terrace:** Moonlight Terrace, a hidden gem in the heart of Ksamil, provides an intimate and romantic atmosphere. This quaint rooftop bar offers panoramic views of the town and surrounding countryside, making it an excellent choice for a quiet drink or a romantic evening under the stars. Enjoy handmade cocktails, excellent wines, and delectable tapas while taking in the lovely atmosphere of Moonlight Terrace.

- **Harbor View Café:** Situated near the harbor, Harbor View Café offers a prime vantage point to watch the comings and goings of fishing boats and yachts. Relax on the outside patio with a cup of freshly brewed coffee, indulge in handmade pastries, and soak in the vibrant ambiance of this waterfront cafe. Harbor View Café is a popular hangout for both residents and tourists, whether you're people-watching or simply enjoying the marine atmosphere.
- **Olive Grove Lounge:** Nestled in a picturesque olive grove, Olive Grove Lounge provides a peaceful respite from the rush and bustle of the town center. Surrounded by old trees and aromatic gardens, this rustic-chic establishment encourages visitors to relax with handmade drinks, local wines, and farm-to-table food produced from the surrounding countryside. Live acoustic music and bonfire evenings enhance the enchanting atmosphere of Olive Grove Lounge, making it a great location for relaxation and companionship.
- **Beachfront Cabana Bars:** Along Ksamil's sandy sands, beachfront cabana bars provide a relaxed atmosphere to enjoy cold beverages and light food while lying on loungers or putting your toes in the crystal-clear seas. From tropical-themed beach bars to rustic-chic cabanas, these coastal places provide a classic beach experience with a Mediterranean twist.

Whether you're looking for panoramic vistas, a tropical atmosphere, or a laid-back charm, Ksamil's bars and cafés cater to every mood and occasion.

Night Clubs and Lounges

As the sun sets over the peaceful waters of Ksamil, the town's dynamic nightlife emerges, inviting guests to a variety of exciting nightclubs and cafes. From throbbing beats to sensuous rhythms, Ksamil's nightlife scene has a diverse range of places where revelers may dance, chat, and chill till the early hours of the morning. Here are some of the best places to enjoy the nighttime pulse of Ksamil:

- **Euphoria Nightclub:** Located in the center of Ksamil's entertainment zone, Euphoria Nightclub is a beacon of excitement and energy that attracts partygoers from all around. Euphoria's cutting-edge sound system, immersive lighting effects, and a lineup of famous DJs create the perfect setting for amazing nights of music, dancing, and celebration. From themed events to guest performances, the club creates an electric environment that keeps the party going till morning.
- **Moonlight Lounge:** Located on the stunning beach, Moonlight Lounge provides a classy respite from the rush and bustle of the town center. The lounge emanates elegance and refinement, thanks to its

gentle, ambient lighting and comfortable furnishings. Guests may enjoy handmade cocktails, great wines, and premium spirits while taking in panoramic views of the moonlight sea. Moonlight Lounge's attractiveness is enhanced with live music performances and themed evenings, making it a popular destination for those looking for a more private and sophisticated nightlife experience.

- **Aqua Skybar:** Perched atop a high-rise structure, Aqua Skybar provides an aerial perspective of Ksamil's dazzling cityscape and neighboring surroundings. The sleek and modern facility has a stunning rooftop patio where visitors can enjoy specialty drinks, handcrafted tapas, and panoramic views of the city below. Whether you're socializing with friends, cuddling up with a loved one, or simply taking in the urban atmosphere, Aqua Skybar offers a refined environment for nocturnal indulgence and relaxation.
- **Beachfront Bonfires:** Along Ksamil's sandy coastlines, beachfront bonfires provide a more relaxed and communal nighttime experience. Visitors may enjoy acoustic jams, unexpected drum circles, and spontaneous dance sessions around crackling fires, all beneath the stars. The rhythmic sound of waves smashing on the coast sets the tone for an evening of fellowship, storytelling, and beachside enjoyment. Beachside bonfires encapsulate the essence of Ksamil's

laid-back coastal culture, providing a fascinating and magical opportunity to interact with nature and other tourists.
- **Club Tropicana:** Located in the heart of Ksamil's nightlife zone, Club Tropicana is a tropical-themed sanctuary where visitors may escape the ordinary and experience the exceptional. The vivid setting, with its thick flora, colorful design, and loud music, takes guests to a fun and exciting paradise. Club Tropicana's dynamic ambiance and lively clientele ensure an amazing night of dancing, laughing, and tropical sensations.

Ksamil's nightlife has everything from high-energy nightclubs to romantic lounges, so there's something for everyone. Whether you're dancing beneath the stars or enjoying drinks with a view, the town's nightlife is yours to discover and enjoy.

Cultural Performances

In addition to its vibrant nightlife, Ksamil offers a rich tapestry of cultural acts that honor the region's creative legacy and customs. Cultural performances, which range from traditional folk music to modern theatrical shows, provide visitors with a look into the heart of Ksamil's dynamic cultural scene. Here are some of the best cultural experiences to immerse yourself in.

- **Folk Music and Dance Shows:** Throughout the year, Ksamil presents several folk music and dance performances that highlight the region's rich musical tradition and cultural diversity. Visitors may enjoy engaging performances with traditional instruments, colorful costumes, and energetic dance that reflect Albania's cultural traditions and regional influences. Folk music and dance performances, ranging from vibrant dance routines to heartfelt ballads, provide a genuine and immersive peek into Ksamil culture.
- **Theater and Drama Productions:** Ksamil's vibrant theater scene offers a wide range of drama productions, plays, and theatrical performances that fascinate spectators with their innovation and craftsmanship. Theatre plays, ranging from ancient works to modern adaptations, tackle themes of love, grief, identity, and social criticism, offering thought-provoking insights into the human experience. Ksamil theatrical performances, whether in little or huge theaters, are a fascinating blend of storytelling, passion, and creativity.
- **Live Music Venues:** Ksamil has a range of live music venues, from small cafés to open-air amphitheaters, where tourists may see performances by local musicians, bands, and artists. Whether you enjoy jazz, blues, rock, or traditional Albanian music, you'll discover a diverse range of musical genres and styles to

fit your preferences. Live music venues offer a vibrant and dynamic setting for mingling, dancing, and admiring the abilities of Ksamil's musical community.
- **Cultural Festivals & Events:** Throughout the year, Ksamil holds a variety of cultural festivals and events to honor the town's creative past and cultural customs. Music festivals, film screenings, art exhibits, and culinary showcases are all examples of cultural events that allow local and international artists to share their abilities and creativity with the community. Visitors may join in the celebrations, take part in seminars and events, and meet other cultural and arts aficionados.
- **Street Performances and Art Installations:** As you walk through the streets of Ksamil, you'll come across a plethora of street performers, craftsmen, and visual artists who bring creativity and expression to the town's public areas. Street performances, ranging from live painting sessions to interactive installations, provide an immersive and spontaneous experience that encourages bystanders to participate and engage. Whether you're admiring a mural, seeing a mime, or listening to a busker's tune, street performances provide a lively and colorful layer to Ksamil's cultural scene.

Ksamil cultural events range from traditional folk music to avant-garde theater, and they serve as a forum for artistic expression, community participation, and cultural exchange.

Chapter 8

OUTDOOR ACTIVITIES

Ksamil's natural beauty and diversified landscapes create an ideal backdrop for a variety of outdoor activities that appeal to explorers, nature lovers, and outdoor enthusiasts alike. From exhilarating water activities to gorgeous hiking paths and cycling routes, this chapter delves into the many ways tourists may immerse themselves in Ksamil's magnificent outdoors.

Water Sports

Ksamil, surrounded by the turquoise seas of the Ionian Sea, provides a variety of thrilling water sports activities for guests to enjoy its pristine shoreline and diverse marine life. Whether you're looking for adrenaline-pumping experiences or relaxing aquatic activities, Ksamil's crystal-clear waters are the ideal playground for water sports aficionados. Here are some of the best water activities to try in Ksamil:

- **Snorkeling and Scuba Diving:** Dive under the surface to explore a world of underwater delights in Ksamil's vibrant marine habitats. The Ionian Sea, with its crystal-clear clarity and rich marine life, provides unsurpassed chances for snorkeling and scuba diving. Discover vibrant coral reefs, old shipwrecks, and underwater caverns alive with tropical fish, octopuses, and sea turtles. Divers of all skill levels may take advantage of guided diving expeditions and certification courses to explore the wonder of Ksamil's underwater universe.

- **Kayaking and Paddleboarding:** Take a kayaking or paddleboarding excursion through Ksamil's calm coastal lagoons and quiet bays. Paddle at your speed, discover secret beaches, and enjoy panoramic views of the craggy coastline and adjacent islands. Kayaking and paddleboarding, whether on a solo excursion or as part of a guided trip, provide a peaceful and engaging opportunity to interact with nature and discover Ksamil's beautiful coastline.
- **Jet ski and parasailing:** Jet skiing and parasailing provide high-octane thrills on the open water for adrenaline junkies. Feel the sensation of speed as you race across the waves on a jet ski, slicing through the surf and completing thrilling tricks. Alternatively, go to the sky and fly above the coastline on a parasailing trip, where you can experience stunning aerial views of Ksamil's picturesque landscapes and turquoise oceans. Jet skiing and parasailing provide safe and exciting

experiences for explorers of all ages, thanks to expert instructors and cutting-edge technology.

- **Windsurfing and Kiteboarding:** Use the strength of the wind to ride the waves on a windsurfing or kiteboarding adventure in Ksamil. With regular winds and suitable conditions, the Ionian Sea is a great playground for windsurfers and kiteboarders of all skill levels. Experience the exhilaration of gliding across the sea while doing leaps, tricks, and maneuvers against the backdrop of Ksamil's breathtaking shoreline. Whether you're an experienced expert or a novice eager to learn, windsurfing and kiteboarding provide a thrilling combination of skill, technique, and adrenaline-fueled enjoyment.
- **Fishing and Angling:** Cast your line and reel in the catch of the day on a fishing or angling expedition to Ksamil's abundant waterways. Whether you're trolling for huge game fish offshore or casting from the beach for local favorites like sea bass and bream, Ksamil has fishing possibilities for anglers of all interests and skill levels. Join a guided fishing trip, rent equipment from local outfitters, or simply bring a rod and reel and try your luck from the beach or a gorgeous fishing pier. Ksamil fishing, with its abundant marine life and gorgeous environs, guarantees a wonderful angling experience for both nature lovers and fishing aficionados.

Ksamil's water sports activities range from undersea exploration to high-speed thrills, providing guests with a thrilling selection of excursions to enjoy while basking in the sun-drenched glory of the Ionian coastline.

Hiking & Trekking Trails

Immersing oneself in Ksamil's magnificent hiking and trekking routes provides a wonderful experience surrounded by nature's grandeur and peace. Whether you're looking for relaxing treks or hard climbs, Ksamil's diversified terrain appeals to explorers of all skill levels, delivering beautiful panoramas and amazing experiences with nature's beauties. Here are some of the greatest hiking and trekking paths to explore:

- **Mount Ksamil:** Climb to the summit of Mount Ksamil, an iconic mountain with panoramic views of the town and neighboring areas. Trails zigzag through lush woods and steep slopes, offering vistas of indigenous flora and species along the route. As hikers ascend the peak, they are rewarded with panoramic views of the Ionian Sea and adjacent islands, making the trek a lasting tribute to Ksamil's raw beauty.
- **Blue Eye Trail:** Travel through stunning landscapes on the Blue Eye Trail, which leads to the mythical natural spring known as the Blue Eye. Hikers pass through

verdant woodlands and gurgling streams before arriving at the mythical Blue Eye, a deep lake whose crystalline waters are brilliant in color. Surrounded by luscious flora and shaded by old trees, the Blue Eye has an ethereal air that captivates tourists and provides relief from the summer heat.
- **Albanian Riviera Coastal Path**: Follow the winding routes of the Albanian Riviera Coastal Path to discover the craggy coastline and secret bays that define Ksamil's shoreline. Hikers on cliffside pathways are treated to spectacular seascapes and stunning views of turquoise waters slamming against worn rocks. En approach, tiny fishing villages, and hidden beaches demand exploration, allowing visitors to enjoy the coastal beauty and peace of Ksamil's Mediterranean setting.
- **Syri i Kaltër Trail:** Explore Ksamil's wildness via the Syri i Kaltër Trail, named for the famed Blue Eye spring at its summit. The road winds through old trees and beautiful valleys, leading to the spectacular Syri i Kaltër, a natural wonder famous for its crystalline waters and hidden depths. Hikers are caught in a sense of amazement and awe as they traverse the tranquil beauty of Albania's countryside, making wonderful experiences among nature's magnificence.
- **Llogara National Park Trails**: Venture into the untamed wilderness of Llogara National Park, where

rough mountains and lush woods invite travelers to uncover their secrets. Trails weave across the park's beautiful landscapes, rising towering peaks and down into isolated valleys teeming with wildflowers and wildlife. The park's paths, from the sweeping vistas of Llogara Pass to the quiet sands of Dhërmi Beach, provide a broad range of experiences that reflect Albania's untouched natural heritage.

Cycling Routes

On two wheels, explore Ksamil's gorgeous landscapes and attractive communities, uncovering hidden jewels and natural delights. Cycling enthusiasts will discover a variety of paths to explore, each giving a distinct viewpoint on Ksamil's natural beauty and cultural legacy. Here are some of the best cycling routes awaiting exploration:

- **Coastal Cycling Tour:** Take a leisurely cycle along Ksamil's magnificent coastline, where pristine beaches and turquoise waters create a picturesque background for exploration. Cycling along gorgeous coastal roads allows cyclists to take in panoramic views of the Ionian Sea and its lovely islands, stopping along the route to swim, tan, and eat local food at beach tavernas. The coastal cycling trip takes you from Ksamil to Saranda

and beyond, providing a magnificent route through Albania's seaside splendor.
- **Llogara Pass Cycling Challenge:** Put your skills to the test as you climb the famed Llogara Pass, which weaves through the steep landscape of the Ceraunian Mountains. Starting in the seaside village of Dhermi, bikers traverse steep slopes and twisting roads to the peak of Llogara Pass, which offers beautiful alpine vistas. With each pedal stroke, bikers are rewarded with panoramic views of the Albanian Riviera and the blue seas of the Ionian Sea below, making the Llogara Pass Cycling Challenge an amazing trip for cyclists.
- **Butrint National Park Exploration:** Take a bike tour through Butrint National Park's historic landscapes and historical sites to see the ancient ruins and natural beauty. Riding along well-maintained paths, visitors may see ancient Greek and Roman sites, pass lush woods, and spot native species in the park's unspoiled wildness. Butrint National Park, with its rich history and different ecosystems, provides a wonderful setting for two-wheeled adventure and discovery.
- **Vrina Canyon Cycling tour:** Take an exciting cycling tour through the harsh landscape of Vrina Canyon, where towering cliffs and flowing waterfalls provide a spectacular background for adventure. Riding along gorgeous pathways, bikers may cross river gorges, overcome rocky outcrops, and see the canyon's

unspoiled vistas. With its difficult terrain and breathtaking landscape, the Vrina Canyon Cycling Excursion promises an adrenaline-fueled adventure through one of Ksamil's most remarkable natural treasures.

- **Albanian Riviera Discovery Ride:** Explore the beauty of the Albanian Riviera by cycling through small towns, olive gardens, and vineyards set among the region's undulating hills and coastal cliffs. Riding down country roads and old pathways allows riders to immerse themselves in the relaxed pace of rural life, pausing to enjoy local wines, cheeses, and traditional cuisine along the route. The Albanian Riviera Discovery Ride, which travels from Saranda to Himara and beyond, provides a unique chance to discover the cultural legacy and natural beauty of this lovely coastal region.

Cycling paths in Ksamil provide a broad range of experiences for cyclists of all skill levels, providing exciting rides across Albania's stunning landscapes and cultural riches.

Chapter 9

DAY TRIPS AND EXCURSIONS

Ksamil is an excellent location for discovering the gems of southern Albania, with several day tours and excursions promising unique adventures and cultural discoveries. From ancient ruins to natural wonders and bustling towns, each place invites visitors to explore deeper into Albania's unique tapestry of history, culture, and landscapes. Here are some of the best day trips and excursions to go on from Ksamil:

Butrint National Park

Butrint National Park, nestled in the beautiful landscapes of southern Albania, exemplifies the region's rich history and natural beauty. Butrint, a UNESCO World Heritage Site, has historic ruins, beautiful wetlands, and various ecosystems that have drawn people for millennia. A day excursion to Butrint provides an intriguing journey through time, allowing visitors to see archeological wonders, picturesque landscapes, and cultural treasures. Here's what to expect on a visit to Butrint National Park:

- **Ancient Ruins:** As you explore Butrint's archeological site, you will discover the relics of a once vibrant ancient city. Discover well-preserved ruins from the Greek, Roman, Byzantine, and Venetian periods, including a theater, temples, fortresses, and public buildings. Admire beautiful mosaics, massive columns, and architectural wonders that provide insights into Butrint's illustrious history and significance as a crossroads of civilizations.
- **Venetian Castle:** Climb to the top of Butrint's Venetian Castle to enjoy panoramic views of the surrounding landscapes, including the Ionian Sea and Corfu Island. The castle, which dates back to the medieval period, provides an insight into Butrint's strategic importance and architectural history, with its high walls, bastions, and commanding position above the historic city below.
- **Wetlands and Wildlife:** Wander through Butrint's beautiful wetlands and explore a diverse range of plants and species that live there. Explore boardwalks and nature paths that snake through marshes, lagoons, and woodlands, seeing a variety of bird species, amphibians, and migrating birds along the route. Keep a watch out for herons, egrets, kingfishers, and other flying creatures that inhabit Butrint's peaceful surroundings.

- **Nature Trails and Scenic Walks:** Immerse yourself in Butrint's natural splendor by exploring its network of hiking trails and scenic walks. Wander through olive orchards, cypress woods, and Mediterranean scrubland, passing old olive trees, wildflowers, and scented plants along the route. Follow routes that lead to secret coves, isolated beaches, and panoramic vistas, providing opportunities for isolation, introspection, and contact with nature.
- **Archaeological Museum:** Learn more about Butrint's history and legacy at the Butrint Archaeological Museum, which exhibits an extensive collection of artifacts, sculptures, and archaeological findings discovered from the site. Discover artifacts ranging from pottery and coins to statues and inscriptions, each of which provides insight into Butrint's cultural past and value as a UNESCO World Heritage Site.

A day excursion to Butrint National Park takes you on a riveting journey through Albania's historical past, natural beauty, and cultural legacy, making it an unforgettable experience for history fans, nature lovers, and curious visitors alike.

Blue Eye Spring

With a compelling day excursion to the entrancing Blue Eye Spring, you may immerse yourself in Albania's natural beauty. The Blue Eye Spring, located near Muzinë hamlet, is a hidden gem with stunning blue waters and unfathomable depths. Here's what explorers should expect when they visit the Blue Eye Spring.

- **Natural Wonder:** The Blue Eye Spring gets its name from its awe-inspiring look, which is marked by an unearthly tint that appears to radiate from its depths. The spring's waters, fed by subterranean rivers and cavernous passages, rise from a seemingly unfathomable abyss to form a dazzling pool that captivates tourists with its stunning beauty. The beautiful colors of blue that ripple over its surface alter with the changing light, striking a spell of awe and interest in those who see it.
- **Journey through Nature:** The journey to the Blue Eye Spring is an adventure in itself, as travelers traverse winding roads and scenic pathways that meander through Albania's picturesque countryside. , green hillsides, flowing rivers, and picturesque towns dot the landscape, providing views of the region's pastoral charm and natural magnificence. As the voyage progresses, passengers are treated to panoramic views

of olive orchards, vineyards, and verdant woodlands, laying the groundwork for the amazing meeting that lies ahead.

- **Exploration and Discovery:** Upon arrival at the Blue Eye Spring, visitors are encouraged to explore the beautiful surroundings and immerse themselves in the peaceful atmosphere. Follow meandering walkways and covered trails to reach the spring's private hideaway, passing through deep greenery and verdant forests along the way. As the sound of rushing water approaches, anticipation mounts, culminating in the beautiful sight of the Blue Eye Spring glistening in the dappled sunlight.
- **Picnics and Relaxation:** The Blue Eye Spring's calm environment provides the ideal backdrop for relaxation and contemplation surrounded by nature. Spread down a picnic blanket beneath the canopy of trees and enjoy the tastes of local specialties and cool beverages while basking in the calm of the surroundings. The delicate rustle of leaves, the calming murmur of running water, and the distant sound of birds combine to create a symphony of tranquility, beckoning visitors to relax and recharge in the embrace of nature's splendor.
- **Photography and Reflection:** The ethereal beauty of the Blue Eye Spring offers limitless opportunities for photography and introspection as visitors strive to capture the spirit of this natural wonder in all its glory.

From sweeping vistas to close-ups of sparkling waterways and sun-dappled vegetation, each frame conveys a tale of amazement and wonder, storing memories for a lifetime. As the day comes to an end, take a minute to appreciate the beauty and grandeur of the Blue Eye Spring, feeling a deep connection to the natural world and the secrets that lay under its surface.

A day excursion to the Blue Eye Spring is a voyage of discovery and enchantment, providing guests with a unique opportunity to immerse themselves in the timeless beauty of Albania's natural landscapes while also uncovering the mysteries of this enchanting sanctuary.

Saranda City Tour

Discover the colorful city of Saranda on a compelling day trip that highlights its rich history, cultural legacy, and scenic beauty. Saranda, located on the Ionian Sea coast, provides a mesmerizing combination of historic landmarks, modern attractions, and Mediterranean charm that entices visitors to discover its hidden gems. Here's what to anticipate on a Saranda city tour:

- **Historical sites:** Start your trip through Saranda's fascinating history by seeing its prominent historical sites, which reflect the city's rich tradition and numerous cultural influences. Explore the remains of the ancient city of Butrint, a UNESCO World Heritage Site with archeological treasures from the Greek, Roman, and Byzantine periods. Wander through ancient temples, amphitheaters, and fortresses, admiring exquisite mosaics, towering columns, and antique remains that provide glimpses into Butrint's storied history.

- **Coastal Promenade:** Stroll down Saranda's magnificent coastal promenade, which has palm-fringed boulevards, lively cafés, and panoramic views of the Ionian Sea, providing a picturesque backdrop for unhurried exploration. Watch as fishing boats bob in the port, yachts glide effortlessly across the turquoise waters, and sunsets paint the sky in shades of orange and gold, creating a spell of peace and romance over the coastal town.
- **Cultural Heritage:** Explore Saranda's thriving cultural scene by visiting museums, galleries, and cultural organizations that honor the region's artistic heritage and creative energy. Explore the Saranda Archeological Museum, which displays an extensive collection of antiquities, sculptures, and ceramics going back to antiquity, providing insights into the city's rich history and archeological significance. Attend traditional music and dance performances, shop local handicrafts and artwork, and become immersed in Saranda's colorful cultural tapestry.

- **Local Cuisine:** At local tavernas, cafés, and restaurants, savor the tastes of Saranda's gastronomic pleasures, including traditional Albanian meals, fresh seafood, and Mediterranean specialties. Savor the zesty tastes of tzatziki and souvlaki, feast on grilled fish and seafood platters, and indulge in hefty quantities of moussaka and pastitsio, all complemented by locally made wines and spirits that represent the region's rich culinary tradition.
- **Shopping and Souvenirs:** Visit Saranda's lively markets and boutique stores to find one-of-a-kind souvenirs, handicrafts, and memorabilia to remember your trip. Saranda has a multitude of items that embody the spirit of Albanian workmanship and culture, including handwoven textiles and ceramics, olive oil, and honey. Bargain with local merchants, bargain for the best rates and bring home a piece of Saranda's colorful culture and legacy as a memento of your visit to this charming seaside city.

A Saranda city tour promises a fascinating journey through history, culture, and natural beauty, enabling visitors to immerse themselves in the attraction and charm of one of Albania's most popular places.

Chapter 10

HISTORICAL AND CULTURAL SITES

Ksamil, Albania's cradle of civilization, is a treasure mine of historical and cultural sites that reflect the country's rich legacy and fascinating past.

From ancient ruins to well-preserved monuments and engaging museums, each location offers a story of conquest, invention, and creative expression, beckoning visitors to embark on a journey through time. Explore the depths of Albania's history and culture by visiting the prominent sites and hidden jewels that distinguish Ksamil's cultural environment.

Butrint Archaeological Site

The Butrint Archaeological Site, located on a scenic peninsula overlooking the Ionian Sea, serves as a witness to Albania's historic past and cultural inheritance. Butrint, a UNESCO World Heritage Site, is a complex tapestry of archaeological wonders dating back over 2,500 years, from its roots as a Greek colony to its subsequent Roman, Byzantine, and Venetian influences. Here's a peek of the gems awaiting exploration in Butrint:

- **Greek and Roman Ruins:** Explore the ruins of ancient Butrint and admire the well-preserved Greek and Roman architecture, which includes a theater, agora, temples, and public bathhouses. Admire elaborate mosaics, carved reliefs, and towering columns that attest to the city's historic grandeur and wealth while also providing insights into daily life, religion, and administration in antiquity.
- **Byzantine Basilica:** Discover the remnants of Butrint's Byzantine basilica, a magnificent edifice with elaborate paintings, marble columns, and decorative capitals. Step into the holy sanctuary and envision the sounds of Byzantine liturgy that once rang through its ancient corridors, providing peace and spiritual direction to the devout for ages.
- **Venetian Fortifications:** Climb the ramparts of Butrint's Venetian fortification to enjoy panoramic views of the surrounding landscapes, including the glistening waters of the Vivari Channel and the beautiful woodlands that round the peninsula. Discover Butrint's strategic significance as a fortified outpost and marine fortress that shaped regional history and defended against foreign invaders.
- **Archaeological Museum:** Delve deeper into Butrint's archaeological treasures at the Butrint Archaeological

Museum, which houses a diverse collection of artifacts, sculptures, and archaeological finds excavated from the site. Marvel at antique pottery, coins, jewelry, and religious relics that provide insights into Butrint's cultural history and historical significance, as well as a glimpse into the life of its residents throughout the years.

A visit to the Butrint Archaeological Site takes visitors on a trip through millennia of history, culture, and civilization, revealing the timeless treasures of Albania's ancient past.

Ancient Ruins and Monuments

Ancient ruins and monuments may be found throughout Ksamil and its neighboring regions, serving as quiet reminders of the civilizations that previously thrived here. From Hellenistic fortifications to Roman amphitheaters and Byzantine cathedrals, each landmark offers a narrative of conquest, victory, and cultural exchange, revealing Albania's rich historical tapestry. Here are some of the notable ancient ruins and sites to see in Ksamil.

- **Ali Pasha Castle:** Perched on a rocky point overlooking Saranda, Ali Pasha Castle is a powerful Ottoman-era castle. Built in the nineteenth century by the notorious Albanian monarch Ali Pasha of Tepelena, the castle functioned as a strategic fortress and administrative hub, with panoramic views of the Ionian Sea and surrounding countryside. Explore its huge stone walls, turreted turrets, and convoluted corridors, imagining the stories of intrigue, treachery, and revolt that once took place within its confines.

- **Byllis Archaeological Site**: Head inland to the ancient city of Byllis, an archaeological marvel with well-preserved ruins from the Hellenistic and Roman periods. Byllis, located on a hill overlooking the Vjosa River Valley, was once a bustling center of trade, culture, and political power, as shown by its extensive agora, theater, temples, and fortifications. Wander through its cobblestone streets, examine its enormous gates, and marvel at its towering columns and carved reliefs as you discover the secrets of this ancient city and its famous history.
- **Apollonia Archaeological Park:** Visit the ancient city of Apollonia, a famous center of learning, philosophy, and the arts that thrived during the Hellenistic and Roman centuries. Apollonia, founded by Greek immigrants in the 6th century BCE, grew to be a famous cultural and religious center, with a renowned school of philosophy where luminaries such as Aristotle and Cicero frequented. Explore its well-preserved remains, which include a grand avenue, huge gates, and a beautiful theater, and picture the intellectual and

artistic triumphs that once flourished inside its hallowed confines.

- **Gjirokastra Castle:** Visit the old city of Gjirokastra and see its towering castle, a UNESCO World Heritage Site with enormous stone walls and fortified towers that dominate the city skyline. Gjirokastra Castle, built by the Byzantines in the 12th century and subsequently extended by the Ottomans, was a military bastion and royal palace for centuries, experiencing conquest, resistance, and cultural interchange. Wander through its convoluted tunnels, explore its armory and jail cells, and appreciate panoramic views of the surrounding landscapes from its tall walls as you discover the secrets of this historic castle and its lasting impact.

These ancient ruins and monuments provide a glimpse into Albania's rich cultural history and historical legacy, encouraging visitors to unravel past mysteries and enjoy the region's timeless wonders.

Museums and Galleries

Visit Albania's museums and galleries to learn about the country's unique history, customs, and artistic achievements. From ancient relics to modern artworks, each institution offers a glimpse into Albania's history and present, leading visitors on a voyage of discovery and investigation. Here are some of the best museums and galleries to visit in Ksamil and the surrounding areas:

- **Butrint Archaeological Museum:** The Butrint Archaeological Museum exhibits a magnificent collection of objects discovered in the ancient city and its surrounds. Marvel at delicately carved sculptures, expertly created ceramics, and gorgeous jewelry from the Greek, Roman, Byzantine, and Venetian eras. The museum's displays provide light on Butrint's historic significance as a crossroads of civilizations, as well as providing a fascinating view into its residents' everyday lives, religious rituals, and creative traditions.
- **National Historical Museum (Tirana):** Visit Tirana, Albania's capital, and immerse yourself in the country's turbulent past. The museum is housed in a spectacular edifice created by famous architect Enver Hoxha, and its large collection spans centuries of Albanian history, from ancient Illyrian tribes to modern-day republicanism. Explore exhibitions on the country's battle for independence, resistance to foreign occupation, and cultural legacy, which include objects, papers, and multimedia displays that bring Albania's history to life.
- **National Gallery of Arts (Tirana):** Explore Albania's thriving cultural scene at the National Gallery of Arts, which has a vast collection of Albanian and foreign artworks from diverse genres, styles, and periods.

Admire masterpieces by prominent Albanian painters such as Kolë Idromeno, Zef Kolombi, and Ibrahim Kodra, who exhibit the country's cultural variety and creativity. The gallery also sponsors temporary exhibits, talks, and cultural events, allowing young artists to showcase their work while also encouraging conversation about contemporary art and aesthetics.

- **Apollonia Archaeological Museum:** Learn about the ancient city of Apollonia and its rich archaeological history at the Apollonia Archaeological Museum, which is located near the ruins. The museum's exhibitions feature objects recovered from Apollonia and its necropolis, including sculptures, inscriptions, and architectural remnants that provide information about the city's religious practices, artistic traditions, and daily life. Highlights include the famous Apollo statue, after whom the city was called, as well as Roman statues, mosaics, and coins that demonstrate Apollonia's importance as a cultural and religious center in antiquity.
- **Ethnographic Museum (Gjirokastra):** Travel back in time with the Ethnographic Museum of Gjirokastra, which is situated in a magnificently restored Ottoman-era home known as the "Skenduli House." Explore traditional Albanian architecture, interior design, and lifestyle as you walk through the museum's chambers, which are decorated with historical relics, household

goods, and handicrafts. The museum's collection includes beautifully woven fabrics and embroidered garments, as well as hand-carved furniture and domestic equipment, and provides insight into Albania's rural populations' customs and traditions.
- **Onufri Museum (Berat):** Explore the heritage of Albania's famed iconographer, Onufri, at the Onufri Museum in the medieval city of Berat. The museum is named for the renowned artist who transformed Byzantine iconography with his creative techniques and brilliant color palette. It displays a collection of icons, holy items, and manuscripts ascribed to Onufri and his students. Admire the meticulous intricacies and spiritual implications of Onufri's icons, which continue to evoke reverence and amazement among both believers and art aficionados.

These museums and galleries provide a look into Albania's unique cultural past, serving as a platform for education, inspiration, and appreciation of the country's creative and historical legacy. Visitors to Ksamil will undoubtedly benefit from the richness and diversity of Albania's cultural environment, whether they are exploring ancient ruins, enjoying modern artworks, or diving into the intricacies of traditional handicrafts.

Chapter 11

LOCAL FESTIVALS AND EVENTS

Immerse yourself in the vivid tapestry of Ksamil's cultural history by attending a variety of festivals and events. From summer festivals that illuminate the shoreline to religious celebrations rooted in tradition and folkloric events that highlight Albania's rich cultural history, each gathering provides a unique view into the rhythms of local life and the sense of community that characterizes Ksamil's identity. Join us as we explore the colorful schedule of events that provide joy, significance, and harmony to both Ksamil residents and tourists.

Summer Festivals

As the sun sets over the turquoise waters of the Ionian Sea, Ksamil comes alive with a kaleidoscope of summer events that celebrate the beauty, vibrancy, and joie de vivre of coastal life. From music festivals and beach parties to cultural events and gastronomic extravaganzas, Ksamil's summer season has something for everyone to enjoy. Here are some of the highlights from Ksamil's summer festivities:

- **Ksamil Beach Festival:** Begin the summer season with the Ksamil Beach Festival, a lively festival of music, dancing, and beach culture that attracts visitors from all around. Set against the backdrop of Ksamil's pristine beaches and crystal-clear waters, the festival includes live music performances by local and international artists, DJ sets, beach volleyball tournaments, and water sports competitions to keep the party going late into the night. From sun-kissed days on the sand to moonlit beach parties, the Ksamil Beach Festival captures the carefree spirit of summer in paradise.
- **Seafood Extravaganza:** Treat your taste buds to the Seafood Extravaganza, a gourmet feast featuring the wealth of the Ionian Sea and the culinary expertise of Ksamil's chefs. Sample a variety of freshly caught seafood delights, such as grilled fish, octopus salad, shrimp risotto, and stuffed calamari, all made with locally sourced ingredients and Mediterranean tastes. Sip chilled white wine or rakia while savoring the aromas of the sea and taking in the lively ambiance of the waterfront, which has live music, dancing, and seafood kiosks.
- **Summer Solstice Celebration:** Celebrate the longest day of the year with this time-honored custom that respects the sun and its life-giving energy. Join

residents and guests as they gather on the beaches of Ksamil to watch the beautiful sunset and engage in traditional rituals and customs that mark the change of the seasons. The Summer Solstice Celebration, which includes bonfires, drum circles, traditional folk dances, and ceremonial offerings, is a time for introspection, regeneration, and connection to nature's cycles.

- **Artisanal Markets and Craft Fairs:** Throughout the summer, Artisanal Markets and Craft Fairs pop up to showcase Ksamil's craftsmen's ingenuity and workmanship. Browse kiosks and booths filled with handcrafted jewelry, textiles, pottery, and artwork made by local craftsmen utilizing traditional techniques and contemporary styles. From beautifully woven carpets and embroidered fabrics to hand-painted pottery and silver filigree jewelry, each piece conveys a narrative of skill, passion, and cultural history, reflecting the essence of Ksamil's artistic community.
- **Fireworks Spectacular:** End the summer season with a boom at the Fireworks Spectacular, a stunning display of pyrotechnics that illuminates the night sky and fills the air with bursts of color and sound. Gather with friends and family on the beach or waterfront promenade to witness the great conclusion of the summer season, as fireworks dance and dazzle against the backdrop of the starry sky. The Fireworks

Spectacular is a perfect farewell to the warmth and magnificence of summer, as well as to another season of memories and moments cherished with loved ones.

Ksamil's summer celebrations are a celebration of life, community, and natural beauty, providing a vivid tapestry of events that reflect the spirit of coastal living at its best.

Religious Celebrations

Religious events have a unique place in the hearts of Ksamil residents, providing opportunities for spiritual contemplation, civic cooperation, and cultural pride. From Orthodox Easter and Catholic feasts to Islamic festivals and pagan rites, the religious calendar is brimming with rituals, ceremonies, and observances that honor the divine and strengthen the links of faith and friendship. Here are some of the main religious events in Ksamil.

- **Orthodox Easter:** Experience the ageless traditions of Orthodox Easter in Ksamil, as the faithful assemble solemnly and reverently to honor Jesus Christ's resurrection. From Holy Week processions and liturgical services to midnight vigils and Paschal feasts, Orthodox Easter is a season of spiritual renewal and celebration, characterized by rites such as the lighting of the Holy Fire and the blessing of Easter baskets laden with symbolic delicacies. Join the celebration as churches are decorated with flowers and symbols, and Christians share greetings like "Christ is risen!" and "Truly, He is risen!"

- **Catholic Feast Days:** Celebrate the patron saints and feast days of Ksamil's Catholic community with solemn processions, Masses, and devotional rituals that honor their religious heritage and cultural identity. Whether commemorating the feasts of St. Anthony, St. Nicholas, or the Assumption of Mary, Catholics assemble in churches and chapels to offer prayers of thankfulness and supplication, hoping for the saint's intercession and the graces of divine grace. Witness the pomp and ceremony of Catholic traditions as colorful processions sweep through the streets, accompanied by songs, incense, and holy imagery that inspire devotion and awe.
- **Islamic festivals:** Celebrate the variety of faith in Ksamil by commemorating Islamic festivals such as Eid al-Fitr and Eid al-Adha, which commemorate the conclusion of Ramadan and the annual Hajj journey, respectively. Muslims congregate for prayers, discourses, and community meals that represent the bonds of brotherhood as well as Islam's core tenets of generosity, compassion, and sacrifice. Experience the pleasure and togetherness of Eid festivities as families gather to eat celebratory feasts, exchange presents, and do acts of compassion and charity for those in need,

building a sense of harmony and solidarity that crosses cultural and religious lines.
- **Pagan Traditions:** Learn about the ancient foundations of Albanian culture and spirituality via pagan traditions and folk practices that have persisted for generations in Ksamil and the surrounding areas. Pagan traditions, from spring festivals and harvest celebrations to fertility rites and shamanic rituals, reflect humanity's deep connection with the natural world, respecting seasonal cycles and life rhythms. Participate in the celebrations as people gather to dance, sing, and give sacrifices to the spirits of the land, calling blessings of wealth, plenty, and rejuvenation for the next year.

Religious events in Ksamil demonstrate the continuing power of religion, community, and cultural legacy, bringing people from many backgrounds together to honor and celebrate life's mysteries and marvels.

Folklore Events

Step into the heart of Ksamil's cultural legacy with a plethora of folkloric events that honor the ageless customs, music, dance, and crafts that constitute Albania's rich cultural fabric. From vibrant festivals to lively performances, these events provide a glimpse into the heart of Ksamil, where community relationships are developed and historical practices are preserved. Let's look at some of the lovely folklore events on the Ksamil calendar:

- **Folk Music Festivals:** Immerse yourself in the vivid rhythms and melodies of Albanian folk music at one of the many festivals held throughout the year in Ksamil and the surrounding districts. Traditional instruments, such as the mournful melodies of the çifteli and the vibrant songs of the lahuta, fill the air with a soulful melody. Local musicians and bands perform, while dancers whirl to the beat of the music, telling stories of love, desire, and victory through movement and rhythm.
- **Traditional Dance Performances**: Witness the beauty and intensity of Albanian traditional dances in mesmerizing performances that bring old traditions to life. From the energetic movements of the valle to the delicate footwork of the shota, each dance represents the area's own cultural background and social conventions. Dancers, dressed in vivid costumes embellished with beautiful embroidery and designs, convey pleasure, sadness, and celebration while performing age-old choreographies passed down through generations.
- **Craft Fairs and Artisan Markets:** Visit craft fairs and artisan markets to see Ksamil craftsmen's artistry and workmanship in traditional handicrafts, textiles,

ceramics, and jewelry. Watch experienced craftsmen display age-old skills like weaving, embroidery, and woodcarving, resulting in magnificent pieces of art that capture the spirit of Albanian culture and workmanship. From beautifully woven carpets and hand-painted pottery to silver filigree jewelry and leather items, each piece reflects the maker's skill, inventiveness, and cultural pride.

- **Storytelling and Oral Traditions**: Enter the world of Albanian folklore through storytelling sessions and oral traditions passed down through centuries. Gather around as professional storytellers weave tales of heroes, villains, and legendary creatures, mesmerizing audiences with tales of bravery, wisdom, and magic. From epic poetry and folktales to allegorical fables and moral teachings, Albanian folklore weaves a complex tapestry of narrative that reflects its people's values, beliefs, and aspirations.
- **Folk Costume Parades**: Celebrate the beauty and diversity of Albanian folk costumes with colorful parades and processions that highlight the region's sartorial heritage. Admire the beautiful needlework, brilliant colors, and complex headpieces of traditional Albanian clothes from many locations, each representing the wearer's cultural identity and background. Folk costumes are a live manifestation of Albanian identity and pride, ranging from the

extravagant apparel of brides and grooms to the everyday wear of farmers and shepherds.
- **Cultural Heritage Festivals**: Immerse yourself in the rich cultural heritage of Ksamil at annual festivals that celebrate the region's history, customs, and way of life. Cultural heritage festivals, which range from grape harvest festivals and olive oil celebrations to summer solstice rites and winter festivities, provide insight into the rhythms of rural life as well as the traditions that connect communities. Sample traditional dishes, see live music and dance performances, and take part in rites and ceremonies that celebrate the land, the seasons, and the spirits that reside there.

These folkloric events are more than just celebrations; they are live manifestations of Albania's cultural history and identity, linking the past and present while instilling a sense of belonging and pride in the people of Ksamil and beyond.

Chapter 12

HEALTH AND SAFETY TIPS

When enjoying the beauty and mysteries of Ksamil, it is essential to prioritize your health and safety. From emergency contacts to medical facilities and travel insurance, being prepared for every eventuality is critical for a stress-free trip.

In this chapter, we'll look at the measures and resources you'll need to stay safe when visiting Ksamil.

Emergency Contacts

Before you go for Ksamil, make a list of emergency contacts who can help you in times of need. Knowing who to call may make all the difference whether dealing with a medical emergency, reporting a crime, or seeking assistance in an unexpected situation. Here are some important emergency contacts to have handy:

- **Emergency Services:** Dial 112 for quick assistance with medical crises, accidents, fires, and criminal occurrences. This number links you with the relevant emergency service, such as the police, ambulance, or fire department.

- **Police:** For non-emergency circumstances or to report a crime, call your local police station or the national police hotline at 129. The police can help with problems including theft, missing goods, disruptions, and safety concerns.
- **Hospital and Medical Services:** If you have a medical emergency or require immediate treatment, call the nearest hospital or medical center. Maintain a list of hospital, clinic, and emergency room phone numbers, as well as directions to the nearest medical institution.
- **Embassy or Consulate:** If you are a foreign national visiting Ksamil, you should have contact information for your country's embassy or consulate in Albania. Embassies and consulates can help with passports, legal concerns, emergency repatriation, and other consular needs.
- **Tourist Police:** Some tourist sites may have special tourist police units that cater to the demands of visitors. These officers can help with tourist-related questions, safety concerns, and language issues.

Having these emergency contacts at your fingertips allows you to seek aid and support quickly and effectively throughout your stay in Ksamil.

Medical Facilities

While Ksamil provides stunning scenery and amazing experiences, it is critical to be prepared for any medical emergencies that may happen during your stay. Knowing the locations of medical institutions, hospitals, and pharmacies may bring peace of mind and guarantee timely access to healthcare services when needed. Here's all you need to know about medical facilities in Ksamil:

- **Hospitals and Clinics:** Ksamil may have a nearby hospital or clinic that offers basic medical services and emergency treatment. Familiarize yourself with the location, contact information, and operation hours of these facilities, especially if you have certain medical requirements or circumstances.
- **Emergency Rooms:** In the event of a medical emergency, seek immediate care at the local emergency room or hospital. Emergency rooms can address a wide range of urgent medical issues, such as injuries, severe diseases, and trauma.
- **Pharmacies:** Pharmacies in Ksamil offer a variety of over-the-counter medications, prescription drugs, and healthcare products. Make a note of the closest pharmacies to your lodging, and make sure you have access to any drugs or medical supplies you may require during your stay.

- **Medical experts:** Ksamil may have medical experts, such as physicians, nurses, and specialists, who may offer medical consultations, diagnostic tests, and treatment choices. If you want medical help, do not hesitate to get it from a certified healthcare provider.
- **Language Assistance:** While many healthcare personnel in Ksamil speak English or other languages, it's useful to have a basic awareness of Albanian health and medical emergency words. Consider taking a phrasebook or translation software to help you communicate with medical workers if necessary.

Prioritize your health and well-being by being proactive about medical readiness and knowing where to get healthcare services while in Ksamil.

Travel Insurance

Travel insurance is an excellent investment since it gives financial protection and peace of mind against unforeseen catastrophes, crises, and interruptions during your vacation to Ksamil. From medical emergencies to trip cancellations and lost luggage, travel insurance may help you reduce risks and guarantee you're sufficiently protected during your trip. Here's all you should know about travel insurance:

- **Medical Coverage:** Travel insurance often covers medical expenditures incurred during your vacation, such as hospitalization, emergency medical care, and medical evacuation or repatriation. This coverage assures that you may get high-quality healthcare services without suffering costly out-of-pocket costs.

- **Trip Cancellation and Interruption:** Travel insurance may cover non-refundable charges in the case of trip cancellations, interruptions, or delays caused by unforeseen events such as illness, injury, natural disasters, or travel advisories. This coverage protects you financially from any unforeseen changes to your trip arrangements.
- **Baggage and Personal Items**: Travel insurance often covers lost, stolen, or damaged luggage and personal items during your journey. This coverage pays for the expense of replacing necessary articles and possessions damaged by travel-related disasters or occurrences.
- **Emergency Assistance Services:** Many travel insurance policies provide access to emergency support services 24 hours a day, seven days a week, including medical consultations, travel advisories, and aid with medical evacuations or repatriations. These programs offer invaluable assistance and advice in handling unforeseen problems and crises when traveling.
- **Coverage Limits and Exclusions:** To understand what is and is not covered under your travel insurance policy, read the terms, conditions, and coverage limits carefully. Pay close attention to pre-existing medical

problems, limitations for high-risk activities, and coverage limits for certain types of claims.

- **Policy Documentation:** Keep a copy of your travel insurance policy and emergency contact information handy during your journey. This guarantees that you may easily access crucial information and contact your insurance company or help services in the event of an emergency or claim.

Before getting travel insurance, thoroughly consider your coverage requirements, compare policy alternatives, and choose a plan that provides complete protection based on your trip schedule and preferences.

Prioritizing health and safety and taking proactive efforts to reduce risks and prepare for emergencies will allow you to have a safe, enjoyable, and memorable time while experiencing Ksamil and its wonderful environs.

Chapter 13

LANGUAGE AND COMMUNICATION

Language is the key to unlocking Ksamil's cultural richness and establishing meaningful ties with its people.

In this chapter, we will look at crucial language tools, communication strategies, and cultural etiquette to help you have a better experience and create real relationships during your stay.

Basic Albanian Phrases

Mastering a few important words in Albanian might help you bridge language barriers and appreciate the local culture. Here are some key phrases to assist you handle daily encounters and connect with the people of Ksamil:

Mirëdita (meer-uh-dee-tuh): Good morning.

Mirëmbrëma (meer-uhm-bruh-muh): Good evening.

Faleminderit (fah-leh-meen-deh-reet): Thank you.

Ju lutem (yoo loo-tehm): Please.

Po (poh): Yes.

Jo (yoh): No.

Më falni (muh fahl-nee): Excuse me.

Si jeni? (see yeh-nee): How are you? (formal)

Tungjatjeta (toon-gyah-tyeh-tuh): Goodbye.

Gëzuar! (geh-zoo-ar): Cheers!

Ku është...? (koo uh-shtuh): Where is...?

Sa kushton kjo? (sah koo-shton kyoh): How much does this cost?

Practicing these words with locals demonstrates respect for their language and culture, which may lead to more interesting conversations and memorable experiences.

Language Tip for Tourists

Navigating a foreign language environment might be difficult, but with these language techniques, you can communicate successfully and respectfully:

- **Learn Basic words**: Familiarize yourself with popular Albanian greetings, idioms, and polite words to make conversations easier and show respect for local culture.
- **Use Simple Language:** When talking in English or another language, use simple and plain language to facilitate comprehension, especially when working with those who may not be fluent in foreign languages.
- **Speak Slowly and Clearly:** Enunciate your words and speak at a moderate pace to improve comprehension, especially when speaking with locals who may not be competent in your language.
- **Use Nonverbal Communication:** When words are insufficient to convey meaning, nonverbal clues such as gestures, facial expressions, and body language can help.
- **Be Patient and Respectful:** Patience and comprehension are essential when speaking across language obstacles. Approach encounters with humility, respect, and an open mind, emphasizing the importance of cultural interchange and mutual understanding.
- **Seek Help When You Need It**: If you're having trouble communicating, don't be afraid to seek help from multilingual people, tour guides, or translation applications. Asking for aid demonstrates ingenuity and a willingness to interact with the local community.

By following these language suggestions, you will be able to confidently traverse linguistic variety and form meaningful connections with Ksamil residents.

Communication Etiquette

Cultural awareness and communication etiquette are essential in generating productive encounters and establishing relationships with natives. Here are some etiquette standards to consider:

- **Greetings & Politeness:** Start talks with a kind hello and use polite words and gestures to demonstrate respect. Address them using proper titles and honorifics, such as zoti (Mr.), zonja (Mrs.), or profesor (Professor), followed by their surname.
- **Personal Space and Gestures**: Follow personal space and cultural standards for physical contact and gestures. Maintain a modest degree of eye contact and avoid invasive gestures or behaviors that might be interpreted as disrespectful.
- **Listening and Engagement:** Actively listen and participate in discussions with honesty and interest. Show interest in Albanian culture, customs, and traditions, and be willing to learn from locals' viewpoints and experiences.

- **Dining and Social Customs**: When dining or attending a social event, follow local table manners, seating arrangements, and meal etiquette rules. Show your enthusiasm for Albanian cuisine and hospitality by complementing the dish and thanking your hosts.
- **Tipping and Gratitude:** In Albania, tipping is optional but appreciated for outstanding service. When dining out or getting services, consider giving a tip as a mark of appreciation for excellent service and hospitality.
- **Language Considerations:** Be aware of language sensitivities and avoid disputed or sensitive matters that may elicit strong responses or discomfort. Maintain a cheerful and courteous tone during interactions, and avoid making assumptions or generalizations about cultural differences.

During your visit to Ksamil, you may develop healthy connections, bridge cultural barriers, and create unforgettable experiences by following communication etiquette and displaying cultural sensitivity.

Mastering the skill of language and communication leads to more meaningful interactions, interesting experiences, and a greater respect for the different cultures and viewpoints that make Ksamil a truly unique location.

Chapter 14

ITINERARIES AND SAMPLE PLANS

Traveling to Ksamil provides a variety of experiences, from quiet beaches to historic ruins and colorful cultural settings. Making a well-planned schedule guarantees that you maximize your time and thoroughly immerse yourself in the attractions of Ksamil.

In this chapter, we'll look at two sample plans: a Weekend Getaway and a Cultural Immersion itinerary, each tailored to distinct interests and preferences.

Weekend Getaway

For those looking for a brief break from the rush and bustle of daily life, a Weekend Getaway to Ksamil is the ideal way to rest, relax, and recharge amidst breathtaking natural scenery and seaside charm. Here's an example agenda for a fantastic weekend retreat.

Day 1: Arrival, Beach Exploration

Morning: Arrive in Ksamil and settle into your accommodations. Begin the day with a leisurely breakfast in a local café or bakery, savoring traditional Albanian pastries and freshly made coffee.

Late morning: Visit Ksamil Beach, which is noted for its crystal-clear seas and pure white beach. Spend the morning soaking up the sun, swimming, and lazing on the beach, admiring the stunning views of the Ionian Sea.

Afternoon: Have a fantastic seafood meal at a beachside restaurant, including freshly caught fish, grilled octopus, and local delicacies. After lunch, visit adjacent beaches such Pasqyra Beach and Gjiri i Hartës, each with its special charm and peacefulness.

Evening: As the sun sets, go along the Ksamil waterfront promenade and take in the magnificent views of the coastline and adjacent islands. Relax with a sunset cocktail or traditional Albanian raki at a seaside tavern while enjoying the lovely ambiance of the evening.

Day 2: Cultural Exploration and Adventure

Morning: Begin your day with a tour of Butrint Archaeological Site, a UNESCO World Heritage Site including historic remains from the Greek, Roman, and Byzantine periods. Explore the old city, temples, and amphitheater, taking in the rich history and architectural treasures.

Late morning: Explore the surrounding Butrint National Park, which is home to a rich flora and wildlife, picturesque walking routes, and panoramic views. Take a leisurely trek through the park to immerse yourself in nature's beauty and calm.

Afternoon: Enjoy a picnic lunch in the beautiful scenery of Butrint National Park, savoring local foods and handmade delights. After lunch, take a boat trip to the Vivari Channel to see secret coves, sea caves, and isolated beaches along the coast.

Evening: Return to Ksamil and dine in a typical Albanian tavern or seafood restaurant, where you may enjoy real Albanian cuisine and regional delicacies. After supper, go around the streets of Ksamil, looking for souvenirs and handicrafts to remember your weekend away.

Day 3: Departure and Reflection

Morning: Relax with a leisurely breakfast at your accommodation while reminiscing on your weekend trip in Ksamil. Take a last stroll down the shoreline, soaking in the fresh sea air and enjoying the tranquil morning atmosphere.

Mid-morning: Check out of your accommodations and say goodbye to Ksamil, remembering the moments of leisure and adventure you had over your weekend getaway. Depart for your next destination, feeling refreshed and inspired by the beauty of Ksamil and its surroundings.

A weekend getaway to Ksamil provides the ideal combination of leisure, adventure, and cultural discovery, allowing you to escape the ordinary and enjoy the remarkable in this enthralling seaside destination.

Cultural Immersion

A Cultural Immersion itinerary is ideal for those who want to learn more about Ksamil's cultural heritage and traditions. It covers the region's history, art, food, and customs in detail. Here is an example itinerary for an enjoyable cultural tour.

Day 1: Arrival and Cultural Orientation

Morning: Arrive in Ksamil and settle into your accommodations. Begin your cultural immersion by visiting the Ksamil Archaeological Museum, which displays artifacts, sculptures, and historical remnants from ancient civilizations that formerly inhabited the area.

Late Morning: Wander through the small cobblestone alleyways dotted with Ottoman-era buildings, traditional dwellings, and historic attractions in Ksamil's Old Town. Visit the Ksamil Castle, which sits on a hill above the town and offers panoramic views of the surrounding area.

Afternoon: Dine on traditional Albanian cuisine at a local tavern or family-run restaurant, including qofte (meatballs), baklava (sweet pastry), and tave kosi (baked lamb with yogurt). After lunch, head to the Ksamil Ethnographic Museum to learn about Albanian culture, customs, and rural life.

Day 2: Cultural heritage and exploration.

Morning: Take a guided tour of Butrint Archaeological Site, led by an experienced archaeologist or local guide. Explore the historic ruins, temples, and monuments that provide light on the region's rich history and cultural significance.

Late morning: Visit the Butrint National Park Visitor Center, which features interactive displays and multimedia presentations about the park's biodiversity, conservation activities, and ecological value. Take a nature stroll across the park, observing local flora and wildlife and admiring the panoramic views of the area.

Afternoon: Attend a traditional Albanian cooking lesson, where you'll learn how to make genuine meals with fresh, locally obtained ingredients. Participate in hands-on cooking demonstrations, hear tales about Albanian culinary traditions, and experience the flavors of your creations at a community lunch.

Evening: Enjoy a typical Albanian folk music and dance performance, complete with live music, vivid costumes, and dynamic performances that highlight the country's rich cultural history. Immerse yourself in Albanian music's rhythms and melodies, participate in the celebrations, and celebrate the cultural richness of Ksamil.

Day 3: Art and Expression.

Morning: Explore Ksamil's bustling art sector, including galleries, studios, and artisan workshops. Begin your day by visiting the Ksamil Art Gallery, which features works by local painters, sculptors, and photographers. As you browse the broad array of artworks on show, speak with artists to learn about their creative process, inspirations, and techniques.

Late Morning: Take part in a hands-on art session taught by a local artist or craftsman, where you may release your creativity and express yourself via diverse mediums such as painting, pottery, and traditional Albanian crafts. Learn ancient techniques, experiment with various materials, and design your masterpiece inspired by Ksamil's natural beauty and cultural legacy.

Afternoon: Take a guided walking tour of Ksamil's lively street art culture, including vivid murals, graffiti, and public art projects. Discover hidden jewels and urban artworks buried away in alleyways, parks, and public areas, each with its narrative and reflecting the local community's ingenuity and passion.

Evening: Take in a cultural performance or live music event at one of Ksamil's cultural centers or outdoor amphitheaters. Experience the vibrant energy of Albanian music, dance, and theater as brilliant artists showcase both traditional and modern artistic and cultural expressions on stage. Participate in the celebration by clapping along to the beats and immersing yourself in the festive mood of the evening.

Night: End your day with a stroll around Ksamil's lit streets and waterfront promenade, taking in the lovely atmosphere of the night. Stop into a local café or pub for a nightcap and engage in interesting conversations with other visitors and locals, sharing tales and thoughts on your cultural adventure through Ksamil.

This comprehensive cultural journey provides unique opportunities to interact with Ksamil's artistic essence, uncover hidden gems, and celebrate the lively creativity that distinguishes this charming seaside town.

Outdoor Adventure

Going on an outdoor trip in Ksamil opens up a world of spectacular natural beauty, thrilling activities, and limitless options for discovery. Whether you prefer adrenaline-pumping thrills or peaceful moments in nature, Ksamil has a variety of outdoor excursions to suit any adventurer's attitude.

Hiking and Trekking Trails

Ksamil has a variety of spectacular hiking and trekking paths that lead through lush woods, steep mountains, and picturesque vistas. Lace-up your hiking boots for an enjoyable trek along these gorgeous trails:

- **Llogara Pass Trail:** Hike through lush pine woods and alpine meadows as you traverse the breathtaking Llogara Pass on the Albanian Riviera. Ascend to the pass's crest, where stunning views await.
- **Vjosë River Trail:** Follow the river's meandering route through green valleys, undulating hills, and quaint settlements. Trek along the riverbanks, passing wooden bridges and traversing rough terrain to see Albania's untouched splendor.
- **Butrint National Park Trails:** Use a network of well-marked hiking trails to explore the park's different ecosystems, including historic ruins, archeological sites, and picturesque vistas. Explore the UNESCO World Heritage Site's unique biodiversity by wandering through old olive orchards, oak woodlands, and bird-filled marshes.

Watersports

Ksamil provides a variety of exhilarating water sports and aquatic activities to suit all preferences and ability levels. Dive into the beautiful waters of the Ionian Sea and enjoy the thrill of the following water sports:

- **Scuba Diving and Snorkeling:** Scuba diving and snorkeling tours provide an opportunity to explore the vivid underwater world of Ksamil's coastline. As you dive into crystal-clear waters brimming with biodiversity, you'll see beautiful coral reefs, underwater caverns, and marine life living beneath the surface.
- **Kayaking and Paddleboarding**: Take a kayaking or paddleboarding journey along Ksamil's calm shoreline, passing through serene bays, secret coves, and private beaches. Paddle at your speed, taking in the breathtaking grandeur of the coastline and enjoying peaceful moments on the water.
- **Windsurfing and Kiteboarding:** Use the strength of the wind to ride the waves with windsurfing and kiteboarding adventures in Ksamil. Feel the surge of excitement as you glide across the azure seas, learning the skill of balance and control while admiring the breathtaking coastline surroundings.

Rock Climbing and Adventure Parks

For those seeking vertical thrills and adrenaline-fueled challenges, Ksamil provides opportunities for rock climbing and adventure park experiences in gorgeous natural environments.

- **Rock Climbing:** Put your climbing abilities to the test by tackling the limestone cliffs and crags that dot Ksamil's rough environment. Ksamil offers an exciting playground for vertical adventurers of all skill levels, from beginners to seasoned pros.
- **Adventure Parks:** Take a treetop adventure at one of Ksamil's adventure parks, which feature zip lines, rope courses, and suspension bridges for thrill seekers of all ages. Navigate obstacle courses built among towering trees and lush woodlands, with panoramic vistas of the surrounding area as you complete each task.

Camping and Wilderness Exploration

A camping and outdoor exploration adventure allows you to experience the calm and seclusion of Ksamil's wilderness. Discover secluded campgrounds, secret valleys, and pristine vistas as you immerse yourself in the natural splendor of Albania's countryside.

- **Wilderness Camping:** Set up a tent beneath the starry skies and spend the night camping in the heart of nature. Choose from a choice of gorgeous campsites tucked around rivers, lakeshores, and mountainsides, where you can enjoy campfires, stargazing, and storytelling in peaceful surroundings.

- **Backcountry Exploration**: Put on your hiking boots and set off on a backcountry exploration expedition through distant wilderness areas and unspoiled sceneries. Trek over steep routes, ford crystal-clear streams, and find secret waterfalls and natural treasures that await exploration.
- **Wildlife Watching:** Keep your eyes peeled for native wildlife as you explore the wilderness of Ksamil. From rare bird species and migrating birds to elusive animals like wild boar and deer, Ksamil's various ecosystems provide numerous chances for wildlife observation and nature photography.

Join an outdoor adventure in Ksamil and immerse yourself in the wild grandeur of Albania's natural landscapes, where every path, river, and mountain has the promise of discovery and adventure.

Family-Friendly Trip

Ksamil welcomes families with open arms, providing a wide selection of family-friendly activities, sights, and experiences suitable for tourists of all ages. Whether you're looking for exciting adventures, instructive expeditions, or quiet moments together, Ksamil guarantees wonderful experiences for the entire family.

Beach Fun and Water Activities.

Ksamil, with its gorgeous beaches and crystal-clear seas, is ideal for a family day of sun, sand, and sea. Spend languid days lazing on the beach, creating sandcastles, and splashing in the calm surf. Here are some family-friendly beach things to do:

- **Swimming and Snorkeling**: Take a dip in the shallow, tranquil waters of Ksamil's beaches, which are ideal for swimmers of all abilities. Introduce youngsters to the delights of undersea exploration with snorkeling trips along the shore, where colorful fish and marine life await discovery.
- **Beach Games and Picnics:** Pack a picnic basket with delectable food and spend the day at the beach with your family. Play beach volleyball, Frisbee, or soccer on the sand, or simply relax in the shade of an umbrella and spend quality time together by the sea.
- **Boat Excursions and Island Hopping**: Take a family-friendly boat tour to see local islands and secret coves along the coast. Board a glass-bottom boat or a traditional wooden vessel and go on an amazing voyage of discovery, where you may swim, snorkel, and explore isolated beaches and underwater caverns.

Cultural and Educational Experiences

Immerse your family in Ksamil's rich cultural heritage and history through a selection of informative and interactive events that will delight and enlighten:

- **Butrint Archaeological Site:** Discover the ancient remains of Butrint, a UNESCO World Heritage Site that provides an intriguing peek into Albania's history. Explore ancient temples, theaters, and defenses while learning about the civilizations that once thrived in this historic city via guided tours and interactive displays.
- **Ksamil Ethnographic Museum**: Visit the Ksamil Ethnographic Museum to learn about Albanian traditions, customs, and folklore. Exhibits include traditional costumes, handicrafts, and relics from the region's rich cultural past. Participate in hands-on activities and workshops that will provide insight into Albanian rural life and traditions.

Nature and Wildlife Encounters

Explore Ksamil's natural treasures and go on interesting nature and animal adventures that will fascinate the whole family. From lush woods to various ecosystems, Ksamil provides a playground for outdoor adventure and animal observation.

- **Nature Walks & Hikes:** Put on your hiking shoes and head into the heart of Ksamil's natural landscapes for family-friendly nature walks and trekking. Choose from several gorgeous routes that weave through woods, meadows, and coastal cliffs, providing an opportunity to see local flora and wildlife along the way. Keep a look out for wildflowers, butterflies, and birds as you discover Ksamil's hidden rural treasures.
- **Bird watching Excursions:** Bring your binoculars and go on a birding expedition to discover Ksamil's diverse avian population. Visit birding hotspots including wetlands, marshes, and coastal environments to see migrating birds, ducks, and uncommon species in their native environment. Learn about bird conservation and environmental care while having intimate interactions with feathery creatures.
- **Wildlife Sanctuaries and Reserves**: Visit wildlife sanctuaries and nature reserves in and around Ksamil to observe a variety of native animal species up close. Visit animal rehabilitation clinics and sanctuaries that care for wounded or orphaned creatures including birds of prey, turtles, and small mammals. Discover conservation and animal preservation projects aimed at conserving Albania's natural heritage for future generations to enjoy.
- **Botanical Gardens and Arboretums:** Explore beautiful botanical gardens and arboretums that

highlight Ksamil's and the Mediterranean region's rich plant variety. As you walk through groomed gardens and shaded walks, you'll see exotic plant species, beautiful flowers, and towering trees from all over the world. Participate in educational activities and guided tours that emphasize the significance of biodiversity and environmental protection in sustaining healthy ecosystems.

- **Nature Photography and Sketching**: Encourage your family to express their creativity and creative abilities by organizing nature photography and sketching sessions in Ksamil's picturesque settings. Capture magnificent scenery, wildlife encounters, and unforgettable experiences on camera or sketchpad to create long-lasting souvenirs of your outdoor travels. Encourage children to explore their surroundings with surprise and curiosity, resulting in a stronger connection to the natural world and a lifetime of respect for its beauty and variety.

By immersing your family in the marvels of nature and animals, you will create unique experiences while instilling a feeling of awe and respect for the natural world in their hearts. Explore Ksamil's magnificent outdoors together, embracing the spirit of adventure and discovery.

Budget Travel

Traveling to Ksamil on a budget does not imply sacrificing experiences or missing out on the delights that this stunning place has to offer. With careful preparation, smart ideas, and a spirit of adventure, you can visit Ksamil's stunning beaches, historical landmarks, and rich culture without breaking the budget.

In this chapter, we'll go over practical suggestions, budget-friendly activities, and money-saving strategies to help you make the most of your budget travel experience in Ksamil.

Accommodation Options

- **Hostels & Guesthouses:** Stay in Ksamil's budget-friendly hostels or guesthouses for economical lodgings that do not sacrifice comfort or convenience. Look for hostels with dormitory-style or private rooms at reasonable prices that include basic services like free Wi-Fi, shared cooking facilities, and social common spaces where you may meet other travelers.
- **Camping and Homestays**: Embrace the spirit of adventure by choosing camping or homestay experiences in and around Ksamil. Pitch a tent at authorized campsites or arrange homestays with local families to experience Albanian hospitality, culture, and customs at a minimal cost. Consider farm stays or

eco-lodges that provide rustic charm and authentic experiences amidst nature's grandeur.
- **Budget Hotels and Guesthouses:** Look for low-cost hotels and guesthouses in Ksamil that provide good value for money. Shop around for specials, discounts, and special offers, especially during off-peak seasons, to find affordable hotels that meet your vacation budget.

Dining and Eating Out

- **Local Markets and Street Food:** To enjoy great and reasonably priced Albanian cuisine, visit Ksamil's local markets and street food sellers. Indulge in street delicacies like burek (savory pastry), souvlaki (grilled meat skewers), and qofte (meatballs) from roadside kiosks and food carts, where you can enjoy authentic flavors at low costs.
- **Budget-Friendly Eateries:** Dine at budget-friendly eateries, taverns, and family-run restaurants in Ksamil that offer hearty meals at affordable prices. Look for daily specials, set menus, and lunchtime offers that provide great value for money, allowing you to eat classic Albanian meals without going overboard.
- **Self-Catering and Picnics:** Save money on meals by purchasing at local supermarkets, bakeries, and markets and preparing them yourself at Ksamil's self-catering lodgings or picnic locations. Pack a picnic

basket with fresh bread, cheese, olives, and fruits for outdoor meals at picturesque parks, beaches, and views.

Transportation Tips.

- **Public Transportation**: Use buses, minibusses (furgons), and shared taxis (shuttle services) to navigate around Ksamil and visit surrounding sights. Public buses provide low-cost tickets and easy routes linking Ksamil to adjacent towns, beaches, and tourist attractions, allowing you to travel on a budget while discovering local culture and landscape.
- **Walking and Cycling:** Take leisurely walks or bike rides around Ksamil's stunning landscapes and quaint streets, which are a low-cost option to uncover hidden jewels and off-the-beaten-path attractions. Rent bicycles from local shops or hotels, or bring your own, for environmentally responsible transportation and outdoor exploration.
- **Carpooling and Ride-Sharing:** Consider carpooling or ride-sharing with other passengers or residents to split transportation costs and save money when visiting attractions or commuting between sites in Ksamil. Join online platforms and community groups that promote carpooling and ride-sharing, allowing you to divide costs and meet new people along the route.

Free and Low-Cost Activities.

- **Beachcombing and Swimming:** Spend your days relaxing on Ksamil's magnificent beaches, where you can soak up the sun, swim in the turquoise seas, and go beachcombing for free. Pack a beach towel, sunscreen, and snacks, and relax on the sand while admiring the magnificent views of the Ionian Sea and surrounding islands.
- **Hiking and Nature Trails:** Discover Ksamil's natural beauty and picturesque vistas by taking hiking and nature trails that highlight the region's unique ecosystems and fauna. Choose from a range of free or low-cost hiking trails, natural reserves, and parks to reconnect with nature while discovering secret waterfalls, ancient ruins, and beautiful views.
- **Cultural and Historical Sites:** Explore Ksamil's rich cultural legacy and historical sites by visiting museums, archeological sites, and monuments that provide free or cheap entrance to budget-conscious visitors. Self-guided tours and interactive exhibitions allow you to see ancient ruins, Byzantine churches, and Ottoman-era architecture while also learning about Albania's interesting history and culture.
- **Local Festivals and Events:** Get involved in Ksamil's lively cultural scene by visiting local festivals, events, and celebrations that highlight the region's music, dancing, and culture. Check local event calendars and

community announcements for free concerts, street performances, and cultural displays that provide information on Albanian culture and customs.

By combining these budget-friendly strategies and activities into your vacation plans, you can enjoy Ksamil's beauty, culture, and friendliness without breaking the bank, allowing you to make lasting memories and amazing experiences on a tight budget.

Solo Traveler's Guide

Going on a solo trip to Ksamil provides a unique chance for self-discovery, adventure, and cultural immersion. Whether you're looking for tranquility in nature, meaningful friendships with locals, or exhilarating encounters off the main road, Ksamil welcomes single travelers with open arms and limitless choices.

In this part, we'll look at practical advice, safety considerations, and solo-friendly activities to help you make the most of your solo travel experience in Ksamil.

Accommodation Options

- **Hostels and Guesthouses:** Look for low-cost hostels or guesthouses in Ksamil that cater to single travelers, providing economical lodging and the opportunity to meet with like-minded people from all over the world.

Choose from dormitory-style dormitories and private single rooms, which offer comfort, security, and social contact, allowing you to meet new people and share travel experiences.

- **Solo-Friendly Hotels:** Select solo-friendly hotels and accommodations in Ksamil that offer safe, comfortable, and welcoming environments for solo travelers. Look for accommodations with great ratings, secure facilities, and handy locations near attractions, beaches, and transit hubs to provide easy access and peace of mind on your solo trips.
- **Homestays and Airbnb**: Consider renting homestays or private lodgings through sites such as Airbnb, where you may interact with local hosts and learn about Albanian culture and hospitality. Choose from a range of low-cost choices, such as individual rooms, flats, or communal spaces, that provide flexibility, authenticity, and unique experiences geared to single travelers.

Safety and Security

- **Stay Informed and Alert:** Learn about local traditions, legislation, and safety precautions before and during your solo excursions in Ksamil. To safeguard your safety and well-being, research travel warnings, weather conditions, and emergency contact

information, and always be cautious and aware of your surroundings.
- **Trust Your Instincts:** When exploring Ksamil on your own, consider your safety and security first. When engaging with people, use caution, avoid dangerous circumstances or unknown areas after dark, and rely on your instincts when deciding on transportation, lodgings, and activities.
- **Share Itinerary and Contact Information:** Before leaving for Ksamil, share your trip itinerary, hotel reservations, and emergency contact information with trustworthy friends, family members, or other travelers. Stay in touch with loved ones with regular check-ins, updates, and communication channels to give peace of mind and support throughout your solo adventure.

Solo-Friendly Activities

- **Exploration and Discovery**: Enjoy the freedom and flexibility of solo travel in Ksamil by going at your speed and pursuing your interests and hobbies. Wander through quaint neighborhoods, find hidden jewels, and immerse yourself in the local culture and lifestyle as you go on solitary excursions and unexpected discoveries.
- **Photography and Creativity:** Document the beauty and soul of Ksamil via the lens of your camera or

smartphone, capturing unforgettable moments, magnificent scenery, and candid interactions on your solo adventure. Encourage your creativity and creative expression by photographing, writing, drawing, or narrating, which will help you to reflect on and share your experiences.

- **Cultural Immersion and Connection**: Interact with people, take part in cultural events, and immerse yourself in genuine Albanian experiences that develop deep bonds and camaraderie. Join guided tours, and cultural events, and volunteer with local groups or community projects to learn about Albanian traditions, customs, and ways of life while also positively impacting the places you visit.
- **Self-Reflection and Personal Growth:** Use solo travel to engage in self-reflection, introspection, and personal growth as you navigate unfamiliar situations, overcome obstacles, and enjoy times of isolation and self-discovery. Spend time connecting with nature, practicing mindfulness, and being grateful for the transforming experiences and insights received during your solo activities in Ksamil.

By embracing the spirit of solo travel and seizing the chances it provides, you will begin on a journey of self-discovery, adventure, and cultural immersion in Ksamil that will leave an indelible impact and inspire future trips.

Romantic Getaways

Ksamil's magnificent shoreline, scenic scenery, and captivating ambiance provide the ideal setting for a romantic holiday.

In this part, we'll look at romantic activities, lodging, and eating alternatives to help you plan your ideal romantic trip in Ksamil.

Secluded Beach Escapes

- **Pasqyra Beach:** Explore the quiet beauty of Pasqyra Beach, a hidden treasure on Ksamil's coastline. Escape the throng and enjoy moments of peace as you walk hand in hand along the beautiful beaches, listening to the soft lapping of the waves and soaking in the warm Mediterranean sun. Find a discreet area to spread out a blanket and have a romantic picnic for two, surrounded by stunning natural landscape and tranquility.
- **Ksamil Islands:** Take a romantic boat trip to the Ksamil Islands, a group of tiny islands sprinkled with isolated beaches and crystal-clear water. Charter a private boat or take a guided trip to explore these unspoiled islands, where you can snorkel in turquoise lagoons, swim in secluded coves, and enjoy uninterrupted moments of romance and relaxation surrounded by nature's splendor.

Sunset Cruises & Sailing Adventures

- **Ionian Sea Sunset Cruise:** Take a romantic sunset cruise around the Ionian Sea to see the spectacular beauty of Ksamil's shoreline drenched in golden colors as the sun sets below the horizon. Snuggle up with your loved one on the deck of a sailboat or yacht, drinking champagne and enjoying delicious snacks as you cruise by magnificent landmarks, hidden bays, and craggy cliffs lit by the warm glow of sunset.
- **Sailing Adventures:** Go on a private sailing expedition with your spouse, discovering hidden bays, secluded beaches, and secret coves around Ksamil's coastline. Hoist the sails and feel the wind in your hair as you traverse beautiful waters, uncovering hidden gems and romantic hideaways only accessible by boat. Enjoy private moments of intimacy while watching dolphins joyfully dance in the wake and seagulls fly overhead against the backdrop of blue sky.

Romantic Dining Experiences

- **Beachside Dinners:** Enjoy a romantic beachside supper beneath the stars, dining al fresco with your toes in the sand and the sound of waves as the music. Choose from a choice of beachfront restaurants and tavernas in Ksamil, each with candlelight tables, fresh

seafood, and Mediterranean-inspired cuisine, giving the ideal setting for a romantic evening by the sea.
- **Rooftop Restaurants:** Enhance your dining experience with a romantic supper at one of Ksamil's rooftop restaurants or terrace cafés, which provide panoramic views of the coastline and neighboring landscapes. Toast your love with a bottle of local wine or champagne while enjoying exquisite cuisine made with locally sourced ingredients and blended with Albanian flavors and customs.

Couple Spa Retreats & Wellness Escapes

- **Spa Treatments for Two:** Indulge in exquisite spa treatments and couples massages at Ksamil's finest resorts and wellness facilities. Soothing massages, aromatherapy baths, and revitalizing skincare routines encourage relaxation, renewal, and intimacy, providing a wonderful respite from the strains of daily life and allowing you to connect more deeply with your spouse.
- **Yoga and Meditation Retreats:** Set off on a journey of awareness and self-discovery with a couples' yoga and meditation retreat in Ksamil's peaceful surroundings. Join daily yoga lessons, meditation sessions, and wellness seminars taught by qualified teachers to build inner peace, harmony, and connection with your spouse while immersed in nature's splendor and the calming sounds of the sea.

Romantic Accommodations.

- **Luxury Beachfront Resorts:** For the ideal romantic holiday, stay at one of Ksamil's luxury beachfront resorts, which provide five-star facilities, personalized service, and beautiful views of the Ionian Sea. Choose from magnificent suites, private villas, or romantic bungalows nestled in beautiful gardens or overlooking hidden beaches, with every detail meant to enhance your romantic experience and leave lasting memories with your loved one.
- **Boutique Hotels and Villas:** Escape to Ksamil's boutique hotels or private villas for intimate settings, customized service, and one-of-a-kind charm that appeal to couples seeking seclusion and romance. visit tastefully designed rooms, suites, or villas decorated with local artwork and fine furniture, and make use of special facilities such as private balconies, Jacuzzis, and romantic turndown services to add a touch of enchantment to your visit.

Ksamil's romantic charm, natural beauty, and magical environment provide an ideal setting for amazing romantic vacations and personal times with your sweetheart.

Chapter 15

TRANSPORTATION WITHIN KSAMIL

Ksamil, located on the magnificent Albanian Riviera, has a choice of transportation alternatives to assist you travel the town's attractive streets, scenic coastline, and other attractions with ease and convenience.

This chapter discusses the various means to move around Ksamil, from public transit to rental services and taxi alternatives, allowing you to discover the city's beauty and attractions at your leisure.

Public Transportation

Ksamil's public transportation system offers reasonably priced and handy choices for those wishing to explore the town and its surroundings. Here's all you need to know about public transit in Ksamil:

- **Local Buses**: Ksamil has an extensive network of local buses that connect it to surrounding towns and attractions. These buses follow set routes, stopping at significant points within Ksamil and the surrounding districts. Bus timetables and routes are easily accessible from bus stops or information centers in the town center. Keep in mind that bus timetables might vary based on the time of year and demand, so check for updates or adjustments before arranging your trip.

- **Minibuses (Furgons):** Minibuses, also known as furgons, are another method of public transportation in Ksamil and the surrounding area. Furgons often travel on predetermined routes, serving major sites like Saranda, Butrint National Park, and other local towns and attractions. Travelers can board furgons at authorized stations or terminals across Ksamil. Furgons provide a low-cost and efficient means to travel between places, with regular departures throughout the day.
- **Shared Taxis (Shuttle Services**): Shared taxis, also known as shuttle services, are widespread in Ksamil and provide travelers with a different option of public transportation. These shared taxis follow set routes and may be hailed from approved taxi stands or street corners in the town center. Shared taxis provide a practical option for short-distance transport inside Ksamil or to neighboring sites, with costs often determined by the distance traveled and the number of persons sharing the journey.

Rental Services

Rental services are a great option for those looking for flexibility and freedom while exploring Ksamil and its surroundings. The following are the major sorts of rental services accessible in Ksamil:

- **Car Rentals:** Several car rental businesses operate in Ksamil, offering a diverse choice of automobiles to fit a variety of needs and budgets. Travelers may select tiny cars, SUVs, and even premium automobiles based on their requirements and tastes. Renting a car allows you to explore Ksamil and its neighboring areas at your leisure, including isolated beaches, breathtaking vistas, and cultural monuments off the usual route.
- **Scooter and Motorcycle Rentals:** Those searching for a more adventurous approach to discovering Ksamil may rent a scooter or a motorcycle. Renting a scooter or motorcycle helps guests easily navigate tiny streets, avoid traffic, and get to hidden beaches and spectacular vistas. It is critical to follow local traffic rules and safety restrictions when riding scooters or motorbikes in Ksamil.
- **Bicycle Rentals:** Bicycle rentals are a popular choice for environmentally concerned vacationers and outdoor lovers eager to discover Ksamil's natural beauties and picturesque surroundings. Several rental

businesses in town sell bicycles on an hourly, daily, or weekly basis, allowing visitors to peddle along seaside routes, explore picturesque towns, and uncover hidden jewels at their leisure. Bicycle rentals provide a sustainable and entertaining way to explore Ksamil and its surroundings while being active and environmentally responsible.

Taxi Services

Taxi services are widely accessible in Ksamil and offer a convenient choice for those wishing to explore the town or visit local sites. Here's all you should know about taxi services in Ksamil:

- **Local Taxis:** Local taxis may be seen throughout Ksamil and are easily identified by their bright yellow hue and taxi signs. Taxis can be hailed at designated taxi stops, hotels, or street corners in the town center. Taxis provide door-to-door service and may be used for short-distance excursions within Ksamil as well as longer journeys to other cities and attractions. Taxi costs are normally metered, however, it's best to clarify the fare with the driver before beginning your journey.
- **Private Transfers:** Ksamil offers private transfer services for travelers who want a more customized and hassle-free transportation experience. Private transfer

firms provide door-to-door service in luxurious vehicles, allowing passengers to unwind and enjoy a stress-free trip to their destination. Private transfers are great for airport transfers, day excursions, and special events since they provide travelers with convenience, comfort, and peace of mind.

- **App-Based Ride-Sharing Services:** While traditional taxi services are common in Ksamil, some passengers may choose to arrange their rides using an app. These ride-sharing networks connect passengers with local drivers in real-time, allowing them to request trips, check their progress, and pay for services using a smartphone app. Ride-sharing services are a handy alternative to regular taxis that provide travelers more flexibility and transparency in their transportation arrangements.

Finally, Ksamil's transportation choices cater to every traveler's needs and tastes, whether you like the ease of public transit, the flexibility of rental services, or the comfort of taxi transfers. By exploring these transit alternatives, you will be able to easily and conveniently travel to Ksamil and its surrounding attractions, allowing you to make the most of your visit to this delightful seaside town.

Chapter 16

ECOTOURISM AND SUSTAINABILITY

Ecotourism and sustainability are critical components of ethical travel practices, particularly in places like Ksamil, where the natural environment is a major draw.

This chapter discusses the significance of environmental conservation initiatives, eco-friendly practices, and responsible tourism strategies for preserving Ksamil's natural beauty for future generations to enjoy.

Environmental Conservation Efforts

Environmental conservation initiatives are critical in preserving Ksamil's beautiful landscapes, complex ecosystems, and distinctive species. Here are some important activities and programs aimed at environmental protection in Ksamil:

- **Coastal Clean-Up Campaigns**: Community-led coastal clean-up campaigns are organized regularly in Ksamil to address marine pollution and littering along the shoreline. Local citizens, companies, and volunteers help to clean up Ksamil's beaches and coastal regions by removing plastic garbage, dumped rubbish, and other pollutants.
- **Protected Areas and Nature Reserves:** Ksamil is home to some protected areas and nature reserves, including Butrint National Park and the neighboring marine sanctuary. These protected areas provide critical habitats for animals, migrating birds, and endangered species, and they play an important role in biodiversity conservation and sustainable tourism practices. To reduce human effects on vulnerable ecosystems, visitors are asked to respect protected areas, stick to approved pathways, and observe park laws.
- **Reforestation and Habitat Restoration:** Ksamil is implementing reforestation and habitat restoration initiatives to address deforestation, soil erosion, and habitat loss due to human activity and climate change. Local conservation organizations work with government agencies, non-governmental organizations (NGOs), and community groups to plant

native tree species, repair degraded landscapes, and build wildlife corridors to improve biodiversity and ecosystem resilience in Ksamil and the adjacent areas.
- **Waste Management and Recycling Efforts**: Ksamil implements waste management and recycling efforts to decrease solid waste's environmental effect and encourage sustainable waste disposal practices. Recycling bins, composting facilities, and trash separation programs are being implemented in public places, hotels, and restaurants to promote recycling, reduce landfill waste, and reduce contamination of land and water resources. Education and awareness initiatives are also implemented to encourage proper waste management behavior among both residents and tourists.

Environmentally Friendly Practices

Adopting environmentally friendly practices is critical for reducing the environmental impact and fostering sustainable tourism in Ksamil. Here are some eco-friendly initiatives implemented by inhabitants, companies, and visitors to the region:

- **Energy Conservation**: Ksamil hotels, resorts, and lodgings use energy-efficient technology like LED lighting, solar panels, and energy-saving appliances to cut energy consumption and carbon emissions. Guests are advised to save energy by turning off lights, air conditioning, and electrical gadgets when not in use, as well as utilizing natural ventilation and daylight whenever available.

- **Water Conservation:** Water conservation measures are being introduced in Ksamil to manage water scarcity and encourage responsible water consumption. Hotels and motels install low-flow faucets, showerheads, and toilets to reduce water waste, while visitors are urged to take shorter showers, reuse towels and linens, and report leaks or water-related concerns as soon as possible to help preserve water.
- **Sustainable mobility:** To experience Ksamil and its surroundings, visitors are recommended to adopt sustainable mobility methods such as walking, cycling, or taking public transportation. Rental companies provide eco-friendly vehicles, such as electric scooters and bicycles, to environmentally concerned visitors looking for alternate forms of transportation that minimize carbon emissions and traffic congestion.
- **Local Sourcing and Organic Farming:** Ksamil's restaurants, cafés, and diners focus on locally sourced products, organic vegetables, and sustainable seafood selections to help local farmers and cut food miles.

Farm-to-table dining experiences highlight seasonal tastes and traditional Albanian cuisine, while also encouraging environmental responsibility and culinary variety in Ksamil's culinary scene.

Responsible Tourism Tips

Responsible tourism ideas help visitors to Ksamil make educated decisions and reduce their environmental effects. Here are some tips for responsible tourism:

- **Respect Local Customs and Traditions:** Learn about local Ksamil customs, traditions, and cultural norms, and show respect for the community by dressing modestly, adhering to religious rituals, and obtaining permission before photographing persons or sacred locations.
- **Reduce, Reuse, and Recycle:** During your stay in Ksamil, follow the principles of reduce, reuse, and recycle by limiting waste, eliminating single-use plastics, and recycling goods whenever feasible. Bring a reusable water bottle, shopping bag, and utensils to help decrease plastic waste and support local environmental programs.
- **Support Sustainable Businesses:** Look for eco-friendly lodgings, restaurants, and tour operators in Ksamil that are committed to sustainability and

environmental care. Choose green-certified lodgings, engage in environmentally aware activities, and support local craftsmen and sustainable tourism programs that benefit the community and the environment.

- **Leave No Trace:** When exploring Ksamil's natural regions, remember to practice appropriate outdoor recreation and wilderness ethics. Pack out all rubbish, properly dispose of waste, and leave natural environments intact to preserve their beauty and integrity for future generations to enjoy.
- **Participate in Conservation Activities:** Get involved in conservation activities, volunteer programs, and community initiatives that promote environmental education, habitat restoration, and wildlife conservation in Ksamil. Participate in beach clean-ups, tree planting programs, and conservation seminars to have a positive influence and contribute to the sustainability of Ksamil's natural resources.

By embracing ecotourism principles, implementing eco-friendly practices, and engaging in responsible tourism behavior, visitors can help preserve Ksamil's natural heritage while also supporting sustainable development initiatives that benefit the environment, local communities, and future generations of visitors. Together, we can guarantee that Ksamil remains a beautiful and dynamic destination for years to come.

Chapter 17

FAMILY-FRIENDLY ACTIVITIES

Planning a family holiday to Ksamil provides several chances for fun, adventure, and quality time together. From kid-friendly attractions to family-friendly services and safety precautions, this chapter will help you create amazing experiences with your loved ones in Ksamil.

Children-Friendly Attractions

Ksamil has a variety of child-friendly attractions and activities to suit the interests and preferences of children of all ages. Here are some of the best attractions that families may experience together.

- **Ksamil Beach:** The beautiful beaches of Ksamil are ideal for families seeking sun, sand, and sea. Ksamil Beach, with its quiet, shallow waves and soft sandy coastlines, offers a safe and fun setting for youngsters to swim, build sandcastles, and play games under the Mediterranean sun. Lifeguards are stationed around

the beach to guarantee the safety of swimmers and visitors.
- **Butrint National Park**: Discover the historic ruins and natural beauty of Butrint National Park, a UNESCO World Heritage Site close to Ksamil. Children will be amazed by the archeological relics of old civilizations, such as Roman theaters, Byzantine churches, and Venetian defenses. Guided tours and interactive exhibits offer educational opportunities about the park's rich history and cultural heritage.
- **Blue Eye Spring**: Experience the breathtaking beauty of Blue Eye Spring, a natural phenomenon located just a short drive from Ksamil. Children will be amazed by the spring's crystal-clear waters, which resemble the brilliant blues of a big eye. Take a stroll along the picturesque pathways, eat a picnic among the thick vegetation, and soak in the serene aura of this natural beauty.
- **Adventure Parks:** Near Ksamil, there are adventure parks and entertainment centers where you may enjoy adrenaline-pumping thrills and outdoor activities. These parks provide zip lines, rope courses, climbing walls, and other thrilling activities for the entire family. Trained staff members safeguard the participants' safety and offer instruction and support as required.

Family-oriented Services

Ksamil provides a variety of family-oriented services and amenities to improve your holiday experience and assure the comfort and convenience of the entire family. Below are some family-friendly services to consider:

- **Family-Friendly Accommodations**: Look for family-friendly hotels in Ksamil that cater to both parents and their children. Many hotels, resorts, and vacation rental properties include family suites, connected rooms, and child-friendly features such as cribs, high chairs, and children's menus. Look for hotels with recreational amenities, such as swimming pools and play spaces, to keep youngsters occupied and involved.
- **Childcare and Babysitting Services:** Enjoy peace of mind knowing that childcare and babysitting services are available in Ksamil for parents who need a break or want to enjoy some adult time together. Professional caretakers and qualified babysitters provide secure and dependable childcare services in the comfort of your own home, allowing you to enjoy Ksamil's attractions and nightlife with confidence.
- **Family-Friendly Dining Options:** Find family-friendly restaurants in Ksamil that provide tasty food and provide a welcoming environment for both parents and children. Many restaurants, cafés, and diners

provide children's menus, high chairs, and other family-friendly amenities, providing a stress-free dining experience for all. Choose restaurants with outdoor dining, waterfront views, or play areas where kids can eat and play in a comfortable environment.
- **Entertainment and Recreation**: Ksamil offers a wide range of entertainment and leisure options to keep your family entertained and involved. Explore neighborhood parks, playgrounds, and recreational facilities where children may run, play, and engage with one another. Attend family-friendly events, festivals, and cultural performances that highlight Albanian customs, music, and dance, offering unforgettable experiences for the entire family.

Safety Precautions for Families

When traveling to Ksamil, make sure your family's safety and well-being are top priorities. Here are some safety steps to consider:

- **Supervision and Communication:** Keep a constant eye on your children, especially in busy or unfamiliar places, and establish clear communication and safety boundaries with family members. Teach children fundamental safety guidelines including keeping together, holding hands in public areas, and requesting

assistance from trustworthy adults if they become disoriented or separated from the group.
- **Sun Protection:** To protect your family from the sun's damaging rays, use sunscreen regularly, wear protective clothes, and seek shade during peak sunlight hours. Encourage youngsters to drink enough water to keep hydrated and prevent heat-related diseases during outdoor activities and trips.
- **Water Safety**: Take precautions when swimming or participating in water-based activities in Ksamil. Supervise children closely around water, use flotation devices as needed, and adhere to lifeguard instructions and safety requirements at beaches and swimming pools. Teach children fundamental swimming abilities and water safety procedures to boost their confidence and awareness in aquatic surroundings.
- **Emergency Preparedness:** Learn about local emergency protocols, emergency service contact information, and the locations of Ksamil's medical facilities and pharmacies. Carry a first-aid kit, important prescriptions, and emergency supplies with you on your trip, and be ready to respond to any unforeseen events or medical crises that may develop.
- **Travel Insurance**: Consider obtaining travel insurance that covers medical emergencies, trip cancellations, and other unforeseen occurrences that might disrupt your family holiday in Ksamil. Examine the terms and

coverage of your travel insurance policy thoroughly to provide proper protection and peace of mind throughout your trip.

In Ksamil, you may create wonderful memories and important experiences with your loved ones by prioritizing family-friendly activities, utilizing family-oriented services, and following safety precautions. From visiting ancient ruins to sun-drenched beaches and cultural celebrations, Ksamil has something for everyone in the family to enjoy and remember for years to come.

Chapter 18

RELAXATION AND WELLNESS

Relaxation and wellness go hand in hand with the peaceful environment and natural beauty of Ksamil, a beautiful seaside paradise.

This chapter delves into the many ways to rest, revitalize, and feed your mind, body, and soul in Ksamil, from decadent spa treatments to revitalizing yoga retreats and tranquil beach leisure.

Spa and Wellness Centers

Ksamil's magnificent spa and wellness facilities will transport you to a world of calm and renewal, with experienced therapists and holistic practitioners ready to pamper and restore your senses. What to anticipate from spa and wellness experiences in Ksamil:

- **Therapeutic Treatments:** Pamper yourself with a selection of treatments and healing therapies that encourage relaxation, reduce stress, and restore equilibrium to your body and mind. Spa services in Ksamil range from Swedish massages to deep tissue massages, aromatherapy sessions, and hot stone therapies, all of which use ancient techniques and natural ingredients to relax tense muscles, increase circulation, and improve general health.

- **Facial and Skincare Rituals:** Ksamil's spa and wellness facilities provide sumptuous facial and skincare rituals to rejuvenate your skin and enhance its natural radiance. Experience the transformational power of organic skincare products, botanical extracts, and age-defying treatments that cleanse, moisturize, and nourish your skin, leaving it glowing, revitalized, and young.
- **Wellness Programs:** Begin your path to wellness and self-discovery with individualized wellness programs and holistic retreats suited to your specific needs and goals. Group seminars, yoga courses, and meditation sessions given by expert instructors will allow you to explore mindfulness, meditation, and conscious living techniques that promote inner peace, balance, and harmony.
- **Hydrotherapy and Hydrothermal Facilities**: Take use of the hydrotherapy and hydrothermal facilities offered at various spa and wellness centers in Ksamil. Steam rooms, saunas, and whirlpools can help cleanse and detoxify your body, enhance circulation, and

promote relaxation and stress reduction. Enjoy hydrotherapy treatments including hydro-massage tubs, Vichy showers, and thermal mud wraps to refresh and energize your senses.

Yoga and Meditation Retreats

Nurture your body, mind, and soul with transformational yoga and meditation retreats in the tranquil setting of Ksamil. Whether you're an experienced practitioner or a beginner looking for inner calm and spiritual progress, Ksamil's yoga and meditation retreats provide the ideal environment for self-discovery and regeneration. Here's what you can anticipate from yoga and meditation sessions in Ksamil:

- **Daily Yoga Classes:** Immerse yourself in the ancient discipline of yoga by taking daily classes at Ksamil's yoga studios and wellness retreats. Experienced teachers lead practitioners of all skill levels through gentle yoga flows, dynamic sequences, and restorative postures that improve flexibility, strength, and awareness. Explore several yoga techniques, including Hatha, Vinyasa, and Yin yoga, and learn about the transformational power of breath, movement, and meditation.
- **Meditation & Mindfulness classes:** Cultivate inner calm, clarity, and presence via meditation and

mindfulness classes presented in serene locations across Ksamil. Discover practical strategies and guided meditation practices for calming the mind, reducing stress, and improving mental clarity and emotional well-being. Explore mindfulness-based stress reduction (MBSR) practices, loving-kindness meditation, and mindfulness walks to strengthen your connection with yourself and the natural environment.

- **Yoga and Nature Retreats**: Immerse yourself in nature's healing energies by participating in outdoor activities, mindfulness practices, and eco-friendly lodgings in Ksamil's gorgeous surroundings. Connect with nature, hike picturesque routes, and practice yoga in stunning environments that evoke amazement, gratitude, and peace. Experience nature's transformational power as you awaken your senses and nurture your soul in its embrace.
- **Wellness Workshops and Holistic Therapies**: Improve your well-being with wellness workshops and holistic therapies available as part of Ksamil's yoga and meditation retreats. Participate in nutrition courses, sound healing sessions, and energy medicine techniques that promote overall health and self-care. Learn about alternative therapies like Reiki, acupuncture, and Ayurveda, which promote physical, emotional, and spiritual balance.

Beach Relaxation Tips

The picturesque beaches of Ksamil provide the ideal setting for relaxation, refreshment, and lovely moments of peace by the sea. Here are some suggestions for improving your beach relaxing experience in Ksamil:

- **Choose a Secluded Spot:** Seek out secluded stretches of beach away from crowds and noise, where you can unwind and reconnect with nature in peace and solitude. Look for secluded coves, tucked-away bays, and lesser-known beaches that provide quiet and serenity among Ksamil's natural wonders.
- **Pack Beach Essentials**: Bring sunscreen, sunglasses, a wide-brimmed hat, and a beach towel to shield yourself from the sun's rays and keep comfortable all day. Bring a picnic lunch, snacks, and lots of water to remain hydrated and fed on your beach trip.
- **Practice Mindfulness:** Be present in the moment and thoroughly immerse yourself in the sights, sounds, and sensations of the beach. Deep breathing, gentle stretching, and mindful walking are all mindfulness exercises that may help you relax your mind, decrease stress, and build a sense of inner peace and presence.
- **Engage in Water Activities**: Swimming, snorkeling, and paddleboarding are all great ways to stay active and rejuvenated while also reaping the therapeutic

advantages of the sea. Explore underwater habitats, watch marine life, and enjoy the thrill of being submerged in the pristine, turquoise waters of Ksamil's shore.
- **Savor Sunset Moments:** At the beach, the sky transforms into bright shades of orange, pink, and gold, creating a warm light over the horizon. Find a comfy area to rest, relax, and take in the splendor of nature's display as the sun sets beyond the horizon, heralding the end of another day in paradise.

In a nutshell, relaxation and well-being are critical components of the Ksamil experience, providing a harmonic combination of natural beauty, holistic care, and calm retreats that revitalize the body, mind, and spirit.

Chapter 19

PHOTOGRAPHY AND SIGHTSEEING TIPS

Exploring Ksamil is a photographer's dream, with breathtaking scenery, ancient sites, and a vibrant culture that provides a limitless opportunity to capture unforgettable moments.

In this chapter, we'll go over the greatest scenic sites, photography tips, and must-see landmarks to help you capture the beauty of Ksamil with your camera.

Scenic Spots and Photography Opportunities

Ksamil is endowed with several picturesque sites and photo opportunities that highlight the region's natural beauty and cultural depth. Here are some must-see spots for taking breathtaking photographs:

- **Ksamil Beaches:** The immaculate beaches of Ksamil are a photographer's dream, with silky white sands, crystal-clear seas, and lush flora producing breathtaking panoramas around every corner. Whether you're photographing dawn over the Adriatic Sea, catching the beautiful hues of sunset, or getting candid images of beachgoers enjoying the sun and waves, Ksamil's beaches provide limitless opportunities for spectacular photography.
- **Butrint National Park:** Discover ancient ruins and archeological treasures in Butrint National Park, a UNESCO World Heritage Site near Ksamil. Butrint's ancient sites, ranging from the grandeur of Roman amphitheaters to the delicate mosaics of Byzantine basilicas, present a mesmerizing setting for photographers looking to capture the spirit of Albania's rich cultural legacy.
- **Blue Eye Spring**: Enter the heart of nature at Blue Eye Spring, a natural marvel known for its stunning blue waters and lush green environs. Photograph the spring's ethereal splendor as sunlight flows through the canopy, revealing the depths underneath and putting a wonderful shine on the peaceful waters. Capture reflections, ripples, and the movement of light and shadow to create stunning pictures that embody the spirit of Blue Eye Spring.

- **Coastal Scenery:** Take a coastal journey along Ksamil's picturesque coastline, where craggy cliffs, secret coves, and panoramic overlooks provide breathtaking views of the Adriatic Sea and beyond. Hike along coastal paths, discover sea caves and rock formations and photograph the ever-changing interaction of land, sea, and sky against the stunning background of Ksamil's landscapes.
- **Village Life:** Immerse yourself in the charm and authenticity of Ksamil's historic villages, where cobblestone alleys, old olive orchards, and rustic architecture make time stand still. Document ordinary moments in the village, from farmers tending their fields to people meeting at cafés and marketplaces, to capture rural Albania's timeless beauty and cultural diversity.

Photographic Guidelines

While capturing the beauty of Ksamil via your lens, it's crucial to follow specific photographic standards to respect local customs, privacy, and cultural sensibilities.

- **Respect Privacy:** Always obtain permission before photographing people, particularly in intimate or private settings like homes, marketplaces, and religious locations. Respect people's privacy and cultural customs by obtaining an agreement before photographing them, and be sensitive to their comfort and limits.

- **Observe Cultural Sensitivities:** Be sensitive to cultural customs and traditions when photographing religious sites, ceremonies, and sacred spaces. When visiting mosques or temples, dress modestly and remove your shoes. Avoid using flash photography or creating loud noises that may disturb the solemnity of religious rites.
- **Protect the Environment:** Use appropriate photography to reduce your environmental effect and leave no sign of your stay. Avoid trampling sensitive plants, upsetting wildlife, or leaving behind litter or garbage that might affect the natural environment. Leave natural landscapes and cultural places as you discovered them, preserving their beauty and integrity for future generations to enjoy.
- **Be Mindful of Copyright:** Respect Copyright Laws and Intellectual Property Rights When Photographing Artworks, Sculptures, and Cultural Artifacts in Museums, Galleries, and Public Spaces. Before photographing copyrighted content, obtain permission from appropriate authorities or organizations, and do not utilize photos for commercial or unlawful purposes without correct credit or approval.

Must-see Landmarks

No visit to Ksamil is complete without seeing its distinctive sights and historic sites. Here are some must-see locations to add to your sightseeing agenda.

- **Butrint Archaeological Site:** Travel back in time to the Butrint Archaeological Site, where ancient ruins and archaeological artifacts provide insight into Albania's rich history and cultural legacy. Explore ancient theaters, Roman baths, and Venetian defenses as you walk through this UNESCO World Heritage Site, catching the timeless beauty and architectural marvels of Butrint's previous civilizations.
- **Lekuresi Castle:** Climb to the top of Lekuresi Castle for panoramic views of Ksamil and the surrounding coastline, including stunning views of the Adriatic Sea, Corfu Island, and Albania's Riviera. Explore the ancient stronghold and its historic walls, and watch as the golden hues of sunset shed a stunning glow over the countryside, offering unforgettable photo opportunities.
- **Ali Pasha Castle**: Learn about the traditions and history surrounding Ali Pasha Castle, which sits on a mountaintop overlooking the beaches of Lake Butrint. Admire the architectural magnificence of this Ottoman castle, which has formidable walls, watchtowers, and

panoramic views of the lake and surrounding landscape. Exploring Ali Pasha Castle's medieval gardens and hidden chambers will allow you to capture its timeless beauty and dramatic attraction.
- **Saranda Promenade**: Take a stroll down the Saranda Promenade, which has palm-lined boulevards, lively cafés, and panoramic views that provide unlimited chances for photography and sightseeing. Wander around Saranda's busy streets, engage with residents, and immerse yourself in Albania's unique culture and hospitality to capture the bright energy and seaside beauty.
- **Syri i Kalter (The Blue Eye)**: Enter the heart of nature at Syri i Kalter (The Blue Eye), a natural spring known for its breathtaking blue waters and magical charm. Descend into the spring's depths, where sunlight filters through crystal-clear waters, producing enchanting reflections and optical illusions that capture the mind and inspire amazement and wonder.

In a nutshell, photography and touring in Ksamil provide a journey of discovery and investigation, with each turn revealing a fresh perspective, a hidden treasure, or a riveting moment begging to be recorded via your lens. Embracing the grandeur of Ksamil's landscapes, cultural legacy, and natural wonders allows you to build lasting memories and share Albania's wonderful character with the world.

Chapter 20

LOCAL CUSTOMS AND TRADITIONS

Understanding Ksamil's local customs and traditions is vital for immersing oneself in Albanian culture and making strong ties with the local community.

In this chapter, we will look at how etiquette, manners, traditional traditions, and cultural sensitivity shape Ksamil's social fabric.

Etiquette and Manners

Etiquette and manners play an important part in Albanian society, representing ideals such as hospitality, respect, and charity. Here are some important etiquette rules to follow when interacting with residents in Ksamil:

- **Greetings:** Give them a warm smile and a strong handshake, and use the appropriate greeting for the time of day. Common pleasantries throughout the day include "Mirëmëngjes" (good morning), "Mirëdita" (good day), and "Mirëmbrema" (good evening). To show

respect, address elders or persons in positions of authority using formal titles and last names.
- **Hospitality:** Albanian hospitality is famous, and visitors are greeted with the highest compassion, generosity, and hospitality. If you are welcomed to someone's house, bring a modest gift, such as flowers, chocolates, or pastries, to show your thanks. Remove your shoes before entering the house and convey your appreciation for the hospitality shown to you.
- **Table Manners**: When dining with the natives, use correct table manners and etiquette. Wait to be seated or invited to sit before taking your seat at the table. Keep your hands visible and do not place them under the table throughout the meal. Accept food and drink offerings with grace, and thank the host for the delicacy of the meal.
- **Respect for Elders:** Respect for elders is deeply ingrained in Albanian culture, and elders are held in high esteem for their wisdom, experience, and contributions to the community. Show reverence and respect to older people by using formal titles and behaving politely and courteously.
- **Personal Space:** Albanians appreciate personal space and may stand closer together during talks than people from other cultures. Respect others' personal space and avoid approaching or infringing their limits during encounters. Use proper body language and gestures to

show respect and warmth while maintaining personal space.
- **Tipping:** Tipping is encouraged but not always required in Ksamil. In restaurants, cafés, and hotels, it is traditional to give a little tip for good service, usually between 5 and 10% of the entire cost. However, tipping is optional, and the amount may vary depending on the degree of service provided.

Traditional Practices

Albania's cultural legacy is rich with old traditions, customs, and rituals that have been passed down through centuries. Here are some traditional rituals that represent the richness and diversity of Albanian culture:

- **Festivals and Celebrations:** Albanians celebrate a wide range of festivals and cultural events throughout the year, including religious holidays, secular observances, and national festivals. Join in traditional celebrations including Independence Day, Saint George's Day, and the Feast of Saint Nicholas, where you may enjoy Albanian music, dancing, and food in a festive setting.
- **Wedding Customs:** Albanian weddings are happy celebrations celebrated with intricate rituals, customs, and traditions that represent the community's cultural

background and social ideals. Weddings, from formal ceremonies to exuberant gatherings and feasts, bring family, friends, and communities together to celebrate love, togetherness, and new beginnings.

- **Hospitality and Guest Relations:** Hospitality is an important aspect of Albanian culture, and visitors are treated with the highest care, respect, and generosity. Hosts go to considerable efforts to ensure their visitors' comfort and well-being, providing plenty of food, drink, and hospitality. Guests are required to express thanks, appreciation, and respect for the host's gift.
- **Religious Observances**: Religion is an important part of Albanian culture, with Islam, Christianity, and other religions living peacefully. Many Albanians incorporate religious observances and rituals into their everyday lives, with prayers, religious festivals, and pilgrimages to important locations serving as displays of faith and devotion.
- **Folklore and Folk customs**: Albanian folklore has many myths, tales, and folk customs that represent the country's cultural identity and legacy. Discover folk music, dance, and traditional costumes at cultural festivals and events, where you can see the beauty and richness of Albanian folk traditions passed down through centuries.

Cultural Sensitivity

traditional awareness is essential while communicating with the local population and participating in Ksamil traditional events and practices. Here are principles to maintain cultural sensitivity while cultivating mutual respect and understanding:

- **Respect Religious Practices**: Ksamil represents a varied and inclusive community that embraces Islam, Christianity, and other belief systems peacefully. Respect religious practices by dressing modestly while visiting places of worship, according to local traditions, and avoiding conduct or words that may offend religious beliefs. Respect religious rites and keep quiet when appropriate.
- **Learn Basic Albanian Phrases:** Familiarize yourself with basic Albanian phrases and greetings to demonstrate respect and enthusiasm for the local language and culture. A simple "faleminderit" (thank you) or "mirëdita" (good day) can help build ties and show admiration for Albanian culture. Locals appreciate the effort to interact with their language and will most likely respond with warmth and kindness.
- **Adhere to Dress Codes**: Be mindful of dress codes, particularly in religious or conservative settings. When visiting mosques, churches, or other religious

locations, dress modestly, covering shoulders, knees, and cleavage. This gesture recognizes and respects local customs and traditions. Consider the cultural background while selecting clothes for social events and gatherings.

- **Show Interest and Respect Demonstrate Interest and Respect:** Show real curiosity and interest in Albanian customs, traditions, and history. Engage with locals courteously, ask sensitive questions, and listen carefully to their tales and viewpoints. Taking a genuine interest in local culture builds real ties and mutual understanding.
- **Observe Social Customs**: Be attentive to social customs and norms, particularly regarding gender roles, family dynamics, and interpersonal interactions. Albanian society values familial bonds, hospitality, and respect for elders. Accept these principles by engaging in community events, eating meals with locals, and upholding traditions passed down through generations.
- **Respect Personal Boundaries:** Recognize and respect personal boundaries while engaging with others, particularly in private or intimate circumstances. When photographing persons or private property, use prudence and obtain permission first. Prioritize people's dignity and privacy, and make sure your behaviors demonstrate sensitivity and understanding.

- **Celebrate Cultural Diversity:** Recognize the variety of cultures and identities within Ksamil and Albania as a whole. Recognize the fusion of influences from numerous ethnic groups, historical periods, and geographical places that define Albanian culture. Accept chances to interact with diverse people, gain new viewpoints, and enjoy Ksamil's rich cultural legacy.

Travelers who exemplify cultural awareness and respect can form important connections, get a better knowledge of local customs, and contribute positively to Ksamil's unique cultural landscape. Nurturing empathy, curiosity, and openness allows tourists to build rewarding experiences and form long-lasting ties with the people and traditions of Ksamil.

Chapter 21

TRAVELING ON A BUDGET

Traveling to Ksamil on a budget does not imply compromising quality or skipping out on unforgettable experiences. With careful planning and wise decisions, you may visit this stunning location without breaking the budget.

In this chapter, we'll look at budget-friendly lodging, economical food alternatives, and free or low-cost activities to help you make the most of your vacation to Ksamil while remaining within your budget.

Budget-Friendly Accommodation

Finding a cheap hotel in Ksamil is essential for stretching your vacation budget without sacrificing comfort or convenience. Here are some choices to consider:

- **Guesthouses and Homestays**: Look for guesthouses and homestays operated by local families, which offer a more authentic and affordable lodging experience compared to hotels. These lodgings frequently offer

clean and pleasant rooms with minimal facilities at a fraction of the price of bigger businesses.
- **Hostels & Backpacker Lodges:** Ksamil is home to an increasing number of hostels and backpacker lodges that appeal to budget-conscious guests. These hotels often include dormitory-style rooms with shared amenities, making them suitable for lone travelers or those wishing to meet other explorers.
- **Camping and Beachfront Cabins:** For nature lovers and outdoor enthusiasts, camping and beachfront cabins provide a more affordable choice to typical lodging options. Many campgrounds in and near Ksamil provide stunning views, modest facilities, and reasonable pricing for tent pitches and cabin rentals.
- **Budget Hotels and Guesthouses**: Look for low-cost hotels and guesthouses that provide good value without sacrificing quality or service. Look for offers and discounts, especially during off-peak seasons, and book directly with the hotel to negotiate lower prices or take advantage of special promotions.

Affordable Dining Options

Sampling local food and tastes is an important part of the vacation experience, and Ksamil has a variety of economical eating alternatives to suit every taste and budget. Here's how to have nice meals without overspending:

- **Street Food and Food Markets**: Visit Ksamil's lively street markets and food stalls, where you can sample a range of local specialties and snacks at reasonable costs. From savory burek pastries and grilled meats to freshly caught fish and seasonal fruits, street food sellers provide a variety of economical alternatives to satiate your hunger.
- **Family-Run Restaurants and Cafes:** Dine like a local at Ksamil's family-run restaurants and cafes, which serve substantial home-cooked meals and traditional Albanian specialties at cheap prices. Look for local favorite eateries with a warm environment, big portions, and affordable costs.
- **Picnics and Self-Catering**: Take advantage of Ksamil's picturesque picnic places and outdoor eating spaces to enjoy low-cost meals in the great outdoors. Visit local markets and grocery shops to load up on fresh vegetables, bread, cheese, and other picnic necessities, then pack a picnic basket for an outside eating experience surrounded by nature's splendor.
- **Lunch Specials and Set Menus:** Throughout the day, many restaurants and cafés in Ksamil offer lunch specials and set menus with discounted rates on chosen items and combos. Take advantage of these low-cost choices to have a great lunch without going overboard, and visit various restaurants to try a range of flavors and cuisines.

Free or low-cost activities

Exploring Ksamil on a budget does not imply skipping out on thrilling encounters and unforgettable excursions. Here are some free or low-cost things you may do during your stay:

- **Beach Relaxation:** Spend lazy days basking in the sun and swimming in the clear waters of Ksamil's beautiful beaches, which are accessible to the public and free of charge. Pack a lunch, a beach blanket, and sunscreen, and you may spend hours relaxing and rejuvenating by the sea for nothing.
- **Nature Walks & Hiking Pathways:** Put on your hiking boots and discover Ksamil's gorgeous countryside and coastline paths, which provide stunning vistas and possibilities for animal viewing and bird watching. Many paths are free to use and appropriate for hikers of all ability levels, making them an excellent opportunity to reconnect with nature and discover the beauty of Ksamil on a budget.
- **Cultural Attractions & Landmarks:** Learn about Ksamil's rich history and cultural legacy by visiting free or low-cost attractions including historic sites, museums, and art galleries. Explore historical ruins, archeological sites, and cultural monuments to learn

about Albania's history and present, and take advantage of student, senior, and family discounts.
- **Community Events and Festivals:** Get involved in Ksamil's lively community spirit by attending free cultural events, festivals, and celebrations throughout the year. From music concerts and dance performances to art exhibitions and street festivals, there's always something going on in Ksamil that provides entertainment and cultural enrichment at an affordable price.
- **Outdoor Recreation and Sports:** Participate in outdoor recreation and sports activities including swimming, snorkeling, beach volleyball, and frisbee, which need little equipment and may be done for free on Ksamil's beaches and park. Join a local sports club or community group to engage in group activities and mingle with other enthusiasts.

In a nutshell, traveling on a budget in Ksamil is both possible and beneficial, with plenty of options for economical lodging, food, and amusement without sacrificing the quality or enjoyment of your trip. By embracing the spirit of adventure, experiencing local culture, and making wise decisions, you can make the most of your low-cost trip to Ksamil.

Chapter 22

CONCLUSION AND FINAL TIPS

As your trip to Ksamil comes to an end, it's time to reflect on your experiences, appreciate the memories you've made, and gain some final suggestions to guarantee a successful vacation.

In this last chapter, we'll recap the highlights of your experience, provide last-minute advice, and solicit your thoughts and suggestions for future travelers.

Summary of Key Highlights

Your stay in Ksamil has been filled with wonderful experiences, from relaxing on gorgeous beaches to seeing ancient sites and eating Albanian cuisine. Here's an overview of the main points of your journey:

- **Natural Beauty:** Ksamil's stunning scenery, crystal-clear waterways, and golden beaches have created an ideal setting for leisure and exploration. Whether you spend your days sunbathing, snorkeling, or hiking

along gorgeous paths, Ksamil's natural beauty has left an indelible mark on your heart and spirit.
- **Cultural Immersion**: One of the highlights of your vacation was learning basic Albanian language and customs, as well as experiencing traditional Albanian delicacies. Whether you've attended local festivals, seen historic sites, or interacted with friendly residents, Ksamil's cultural diversity has increased your enthusiasm for this dynamic location.
- **Adventures and Activities:** Ksamil boasts a wide choice of activities to suit every interest and inclination, including water sports and outdoor adventures, cultural tours, and gourmet experiences. Whether you've taken a day excursion to Butrint National Park, investigated the Blue Eye Spring, or simply strolled along the Saranda Promenade, your days have been full of adventure and discovery.
- **Budget-Friendly Options:** With so many inexpensive lodging, eating, and entertainment options in Ksamil, budget travel has become both doable and pleasurable. By making wise decisions and embracing local culture, you've been able to stretch your vacation budget without sacrificing quality or experience.

Last Minute Recommendations

As you prepare to say goodbye to Ksamil, here are some last-minute suggestions for making the most of your remaining time:

- **Capture Memories:** Document your journey with pictures, diary notes, or sketches. Document the sights, sounds, and events that made your vacation to Ksamil remarkable, and save these memories for years.
- **Savor Local Flavors:** Enjoy one last dinner of authentic Albanian cuisine, including baklava, burek, and fresh fish. Visit a local market to purchase souvenirs and gastronomic delicacies to take home a taste of Ksamil.
- **Reflect and Relax:** Take some time to reflect on your journey and the lessons you've learned along the way. Find a quiet location by the beach or in a peaceful garden to rest, unwind, and take in the beauty and peacefulness of Ksamil one final time before leaving.
- **Exchange Contact Information:** Share contact information with newfound friends and fellow travelers, building ties that may last beyond the duration of your trip. Share your memories, travel advice, and contact information to remain in touch and reconnect in the future.

- **Plan Your Next Adventure:** As you say goodbye to Ksamil, let the spirit of adventure lead you to your next destination. Whether you're exploring other parts of Albania, going on a new foreign journey, or planning a return trip to Ksamil, let your wanderlust guide you to new vistas and experiences.

Feedback and Suggestions

We appreciate your input and recommendations for improving the travel experience for future guests to Ksamil. Whether you've overcome obstacles, uncover hidden treasures, or have suggestions for improvement, we urge you to offer your views and observations to help define the future of tourism in Ksamil and beyond.

- **Feedback**: Share your feedback on accommodation, dining, attractions, and services encountered during your stay in Ksamil. Highlight areas of excellence, highlight areas for development, and offer constructive feedback to assist local businesses and tourist providers improve the guest experience.
- **Recommendations:** Make recommendations for new experiences, activities, or facilities that will improve the travel experience in Ksamil. Your recommendations, whether they are about extending eco-friendly activities, boosting cultural events, or

enhancing accessibility for tourists of all abilities, will help Ksamil become a more inclusive and sustainable tourism destination.

- **Community Engagement:** Participate in community engagement programs that help local organizations, conservation efforts, and cultural preservation projects in Ksamil. Whether you volunteer, donate, or participate in community activities, your actions may have a significant influence on the lives of locals as well as the destination's sustainability.

As you wrap up your trip to Ksamil, remember that the memories and experiences you've gained will be with you long after you've gone home. May your trips be filled with adventure, discovery, and joy, and may Ksamil's energy inspire your wanderlust for years to come. Safe travels, and until we meet again in Ksamil or wherever your path leads you!

Appendix

USEFUL RESOURCES

This appendix contains a variety of useful materials to help you improve your trip experience in Ksamil. These resources, which include emergency contact information, navigational tools, and language resources, can help you manage your travel with confidence and ease.

Emergency Contacts

During your stay in Ksamil, it is important to become acquainted with emergency contacts to receive prompt aid in the event of an unanticipated crisis. Here are some crucial figures to have handy:

- **Emergency Services:** Dial 112 if you need police, ambulance, or fire services.
- **Tourist Police:** Contact the Tourist Police for support and advice customized to tourists' requirements. Tel: 129.
- **Medical Emergencies**: In the event of a medical emergency, call the nearest hospital or medical

institution. For non-emergency medical help, contact the Medical Center in Ksamil at +355 69 505 4422.

Maps and Navigational Tools

Maps and navigational aids make it easy to navigate Ksamil's streets and attractions. Here are some resources to help you.

- **Google Maps:** Available both online and offline, Google Maps offers extensive maps, directions, and sites of interest in Ksamil and the surrounding areas. www.maps.google.com
- **Maps.me**: An easy-to-use offline mapping program that allows you to download comprehensive maps of Ksamil and travel without the internet. www.maps.me
- **Ksamil Tourist Map**: Get a free tourist map from local tourist information centers or hotels that highlight Ksamil's main attractions, landmarks, and services.

Additional Reading and References

Add to your understanding of Ksamil and Albania with extra reading resources and references. Here are a few recommended resources:

- **Lonely Planet Albania:** A comprehensive travel guidebook that discusses Ksamil's attractions, history, culture, and practical travel suggestions. www.lonelyplanet.com/albania
- **National Geographic Traveler Albania:** Discover Albania's natural beauty, cultural treasures, and off-the-beaten-path sites via magnificent photography and compelling anecdotes. www.nationalgeographic.com/travel/albania
- **Albanian Tourism Board:** Check out the Albanian Tourism Board's official website for the latest information on events, activities, and travel in Ksamil and around Albania. www.albania.al

Useful Local Phrases

Learning some important Albanian words will allow you to immerse yourself in local culture and interact with the people of Ksamil. Here are a few sentences to help you start:

Mirëdita: Good day!

Faleminderit: Thank you.

Po: Yes

Jo: No

Mirmbajtje: Goodbye

Ku është...? - Where is...?

Sa kushton kjo: How much does this cost?

Ju lutem: Please!

Tungjatjeta: Hi.

Lutem: Pardon me.

During your stay in Ksamil, use these terms to improve communication while still respecting the local language and customs.

Addresses and Locations for Popular Accommodation

Finding suitable lodging is essential for a good stay in Ksamil. Here are several popular hotels, resorts, and guesthouses, with addresses and locations:

Hotel Riviera: Situated on the seafront, Hotel Riviera provides breathtaking views of the Ionian Sea. Address: Rruga Pavaresia in Ksamil. Website: www.hotelrivieraksamil.com.

Vila Relax: A beautiful guesthouse situated on lush grounds, Vila Relax offers a tranquil refuge close to Ksamil's attractions. Address: Rruga Butrinti in Ksamil.

Website address: www.vilarelaxksamil.com.

Ksamil Apartments: Ksamil Apartments provides self-catering rooms with contemporary conveniences and is located near the beach and town center. Address: Rruga Ismail Kadare in Ksamil.

Website address: www.ksamilapartments.com.

Hotel Castle Park: Located among olive orchards, Hotel Castle Park provides nice accommodations and a relaxing ambiance. Address: Rruga Sarande-Butrint, Ksamil.

Website address: www.hotelcastlepark.com.

Villa Blu Guesthouse: A family-run establishment with a warm atmosphere and customized service. Address: Rruga Manastiri in Ksamil.

Website address: www.villablucksamil.com

Addresses and Locations for Popular Restaurants and Cafes

At these renowned Ksamil restaurants and cafés, you may enjoy the different tastes of Albanian cuisine as well as international dishes.

Limanaki Restaurant: Enjoy fresh seafood and Mediterranean dishes with panoramic sea views at Limanaki

Restaurant. Address: Ksamil Beach in Ksamil. Website address: www.limanakirestaurant.com.

Restaurant Agimi: Serving traditional Albanian food in a comfortable setting, Restaurant Agimi is popular with both residents and visitors. Address: Rruga Jonia in Ksamil.

Cafe Bar Porto: Relax with a cup of coffee or a refreshing drink at Cafe Bar Porto, which is located on the waterfront promenade. Address: Rruga Ismail Kadare in Ksamil.

Piceri Ristorante Pronto: Indulge in delicious wood-fired pizzas and Italian specialties at Piceri Ristorante Pronto. Address: Rruga Pavaresia in Ksamil.

Cafe Relax: Unwind and mingle at Cafe Relax, which is noted for its laid-back environment and beautiful views. Address: Rruga Sarande-Butrint, Ksamil.

Addresses and Locations for Popular Bars and Clubs

Enjoy Ksamil's lively nightlife scene at these renowned bars and clubs:

Bar Sunset: Enjoy cocktails and live music as you watch the sunset over the Adriatic Sea at Bar Sunset. Address: Rruga Jonia in Ksamil.

Club Euforia: Dance the night away to the newest sounds and DJ sets at Club Euforia, a vibrant nightclub in the center of Ksamil. Address: Rruga Sarande-Butrint, Ksamil.

Bar Shqiponja: A cozy bar with a relaxed atmosphere, Bar Shqiponja is perfect for enjoying drinks with friends. Address: Rruga Pavaresia in Ksamil.

Summer Beach Bar: Summer Beach Bar, located close to the beach, serves cool cocktails and has a seaside ambiance throughout the day and night. Address: Ksamil Beach in Ksamil.

Bar Cuba Libre: Sip unique cocktails and enjoy the vibrant atmosphere at Bar Cuba Libre, a favorite destination for both locals and visitors. Address: Rruga Ismail Kadare in Ksamil.

Addresses and locations of major attractions

Discover the beauty and history of Ksamil through these major attractions and landmarks:

Ksamil Islands: Take a boat excursion to discover the beautiful Ksamil Islands, which are famed for their clean beaches and turquoise waters.

Butrint National Park: Explore the historic remains of Butrint, a UNESCO World Heritage Site with Greek, Roman, and Byzantine architecture. Address: Butrint, Ksamil.

Website address: www.butrint.org .

Blue Eye Spring: Behold the breathtaking Blue Eye Spring, a natural wonder with crystal-clear blue waters and verdant surrounds. Address: Blue Eye, Ksamil.

Lekursi Castle: Climb to the top of Lekursi Castle for stunning views over Ksamil, Saranda, and the Ionian shoreline. Address is Lekursi, Ksamil.

Syri i Kalter Beach: Unwind and swim in the lovely waters of Syri i Kalter Beach, which is named after a stunning blue eye spring. Address: Syri i Kalter, Kamil.

Map of Ksamil, Albania

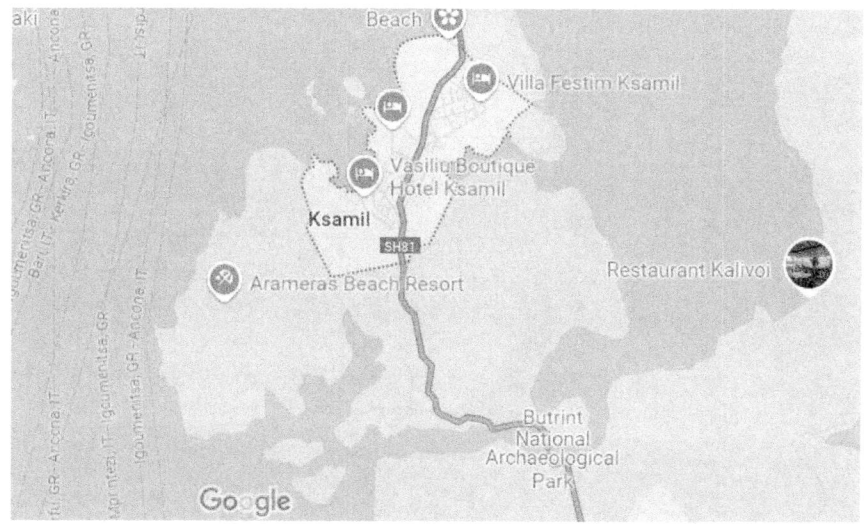

https://maps.app.goo.gl/UyhA5ZeRBSZ7cpie7

SCAN IMAGE / QR CODE WITH YOUR PHONE

TO GET THE LOCATIONS IN REAL TIME

Map of Restaurants

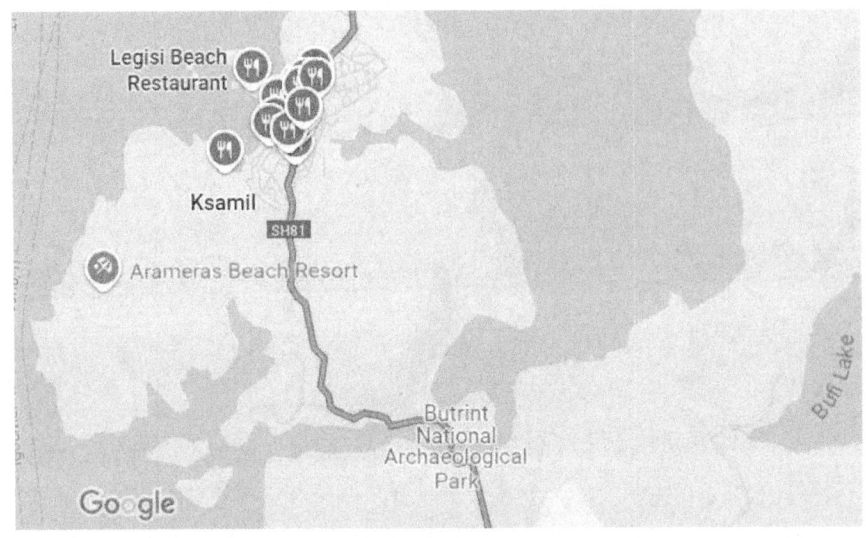

https://maps.app.goo.gl/9ta9rbjvoceXLf5F6

SCAN IMAGE / QR CODE WITH YOUR PHONE

TO GET THE LOCATIONS IN REAL TIME

Map of Things to Do in Ksamil

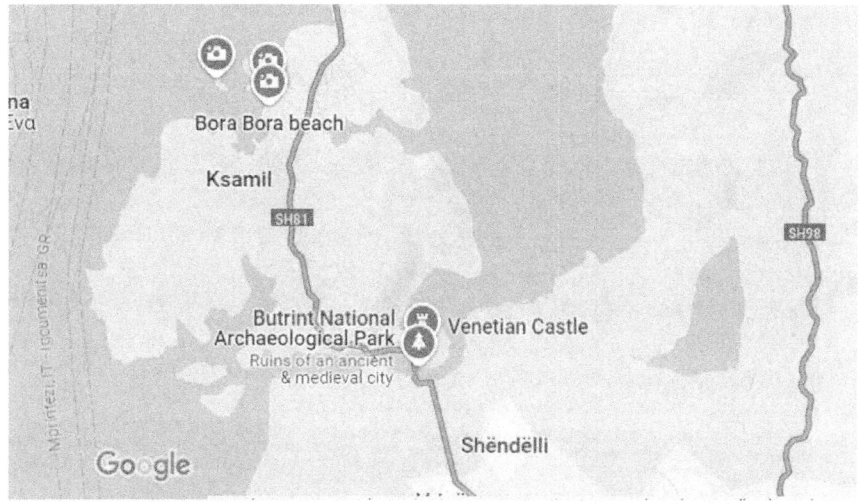

https://maps.app.goo.gl/2ALLAzPPnvDydv6U6

SCAN IMAGE / QR CODE WITH YOUR PHONE

TO GET THE LOCATIONS IN REAL TIME

Map of Museums

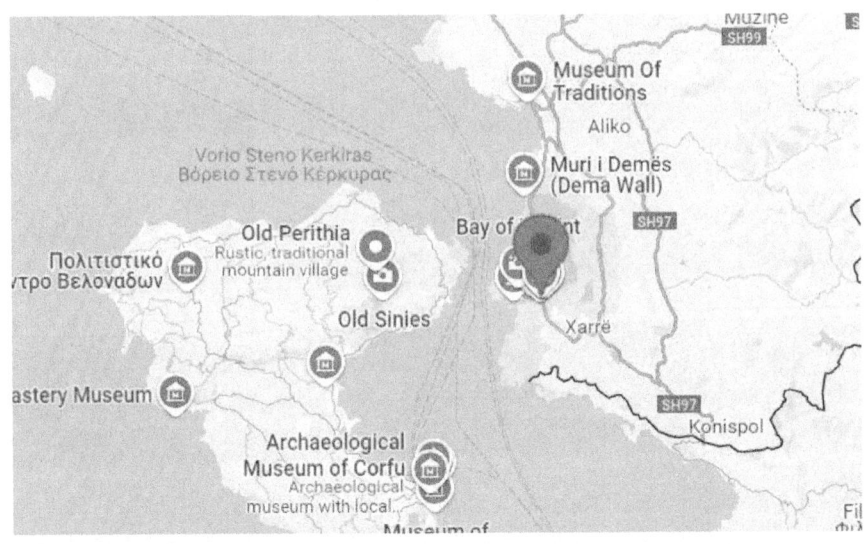

https://maps.app.goo.gl/SM6bvXLQCLHfGGgT6

SCAN IMAGE / QR CODE WITH YOUR PHONE

TO GET THE LOCATIONS IN REAL TIME

Printed in Great Britain
by Amazon